Table of Contents

When we talk about the Arctic, it is an area that is going to become hugely important to us as a nation.[1]

—U.S. Chief of Naval Operations, Admiral Gary Roughhead, 16 June 2011

Chapter I: Introduction

The United States military is no stranger to change. It has reconfigured a number of times since its inception. A number of forces have driven these changes. Sometimes existential threats have been the driving force, such as the dramatic build-ups prior to WWI and WWII. In other cases, the military attempts to provide an answer to global challenges—such as the changes in the international power structure leading to the Cold War, as well as the period following 11 September 2001. Technology has also been seen as a major driver in military change.[2] And, occasionally, the United States has assumed an increase in responsibilities in a geographic region. This monograph is concerned with the last type—a geo-environmental change.

The United States military now faces the prospect of increased responsibility in the Arctic region, where a variety of changes is now emerging.[3] How the United States adapts to these challenges could have long-lasting ramifications for national security. This is due, in part, to the strategic importance of the Arctic.

---

[1] United States Navy, "Chief of Naval Operations (CNO) Admiral Gary Roughhead speaks at Active in the Arctic Seminar," www.navy.mil, 16 June 2011, http://www.navy.mil/navydata/people/cno/Roughhead/Speech/110616%20Arctic%20Capitol%20Hill.pdf (accessed 13 September 2011). Italics mine.

[2] Clifford J. Rogers, "'As If a New Sun had Arisen': England's Fourteenth-century RMA," in *The Dynamics of Military Revolution 1300–2050,* eds. MacGregor Knox and Williamson Murray (New York: Cambridge University Press, 2009), 18.

[3] This monograph uses the definition of the Arctic in the Department of Defense's *Report to Congress on Arctic Operations and the Northwest Passage.* It states, "For this report, the Arctic is defined as that region which encompasses all U.S. and foreign territory north of the Arctic Circle and all U.S. territory north and west of the boundary formed by the Porcupine, Yukon, and Kuskokwim Rivers, and all contiguous seas and straits north of and adjacent to the Arctic Circle. This definition is consistent with the Arctic Research and Policy Act of 1984 (15 U.S.C. 4111) and Arctic Council usage." Department of Defense, *Report to Congress on Arctic Operations and the Northwest Passage*, DoD Report to Congress, May 2011, http://www.defense.gov/pubs/pdfs/Tab_A_Arctic_Report_Public.pdf (accessed 13 September 2011), 2.

Importance of the Arctic

The Arctic is a region of growing importance in large part owing to the effects of climate change which is melting the Arctic sea ice. According to Heather Conley and Jamie Kraut, "The polar ice cap today is 25 percent smaller than it was in 1978."[4] And the rate of warming in the Arctic seems to be increasing. A 2011 AMAP (Arctic Monitoring and Assessment Programme) report states, "The past six years (2005–2010) have been the warmest period ever recorded in the Arctic."[5] The ramifications of these changes in the Arctic are far-reaching. According to Ronald O'Rourke, an analyst for the Congressional Research Service, a potential large-scale reduction of ice in the Arctic "opens opportunities for transport through the Northwest Passage and the Northern Sea Route, extraction of potential oil and gas resources, and expanded fishing and tourism."[6]

The Arctic's vast natural resources contribute to its importance. According to the U.S. Geological Survey, "The extensive Arctic continental shelves may constitute the geographically largest unexplored prospective area for petroleum remaining on Earth."[7] In a world of limited

---

[4] Heather Conley and Jamie Kraut, *U.S. Strategic Interests in the Arctic: An Assessment of Current Challenges and New Opportunities for Cooperation*, Center for Strategic and International Studies, April 2010, http://csis.org/files/publication/100426_Conley_USStrategicInterests_Web.pdf (accessed 11 September 2011), 1.

[5] AMAP (Arctic Monitoring and Assessment Programme) Secretariat, *Snow, Water, Ice and Permafrost in the Arctic*, 2011, http://s3.documentcloud.org/documents/88367/arctic-ice-melt-2011-executivesummary.pdf (accessed September 11, 2011), 4. The original text was italicized. AMAP is "a programme group of the Arctic Council." AMAP Secretariat, "AMAP: Arctic Monitoring and Assessment Programme," http://www.amap.no/ (accessed 11 September 2011). See also, Mark Boslough et al., "The Arctic as a Test Case for an Assessment of Climate Impacts on National Security," *Sandia*, November 2008, http://est.sandia.gov/earth/docs/SAND2008-7006.pdf (accessed September 11, 2011), 3. The authors note that, "Parts of Alaska, western Canada, and Siberia are currently warming at twice the global rate."

[6] Ronald O'Rourke, *Changes in the Arctic: Background and Issues for Congress,* CRS Report for Congress (Washington D.C.: Congressional Research Service, 7 April 2011), 8.

[7] Kenneth J. Bird et al., "Circum-Arctic Resource Appraisal: Estimates of Undiscovered Oil and Gas North of the Arctic Circle," (USGS Fact Sheet 2008-3049) *USGS*, 2008, http://pubs.usgs.gov/fs/2008/3049/ (accessed 7 February 2012), 1.; See also, U.S. Geological Survey, "90 Billion Barrels of Oil and 1,670 Trillion Cubic Feet of Natural Gas Assessed in the Arctic," 23 July 2008, http://www.usgs.gov/newsroom/article.asp?ID=1980&from=rss_home (accessed 12 September 2011). This

resources, this represents a region of great possibilities for Arctic stakeholders. And the countries with coastal areas in the Arctic (Canada, Denmark via Greenland, Norway, the Russian Federation, and the United States via Alaska)—also known as the "Arctic 5"—take their interests in the Arctic seriously. Various Arctic countries have generated claims for the extension of their Exclusive Economic Zones under the United Nations Convention on the Law of the Seas (UNCLOS),[8] and not always without controversy. For example, Russia's unsettled claim for the undersea Lomonosov Ridge competes with a Canadian claim.[9] But proximity to the Arctic does not place Arctic coastal states in an exclusive "members only" club. Even non-Arctic countries are interested in the region,[10] further underscoring the importance of the region—as well as its possibilities.

The area above the Arctic's surface generates controversy as well. There are disagreements over land and sea boundaries as well as rights of passage.[11] For example, Canada asserts that the Northwest Passage, which passes through her northern islands, comprises Canadian national waters, while other actors state that the Northwest Passage is an international strait.[12]

---

report identifies that petroleum resources in the Arctic "account for about 22 percent of the undiscovered, technically recoverable resources in the world."

[8] O'Rourke, *Changes in the Arctic*, 11. O'Rourke notes that the United States is not a party to UNCLOS and "cannot submit a claim under Article 76."

[9] Ibid.

[10] Conley and Kraut, *U.S. Strategic Interests*, 14. Conley and Kraut note that, "Highlighting the Arctic's growing global importance, a number of countries with no geographical links to the Arctic region but with important commercial and economic interests, such as China, South Korea, and the European Union, want to have a voice in future Arctic deliberations. France, Germany, Poland, Spain, the Netherlands, and the United Kingdom have been granted 'permanent observer' status on the Arctic Council, and China is considered an 'ad hoc observer.'"

[11] O'Rourke, *Changes in the Arctic*, 11–12.

[12] Ibid., 11.

A potential increase in U.S. commercial traffic in the Arctic also translates to a possible increase in responsibilities for the United States. This increase in traffic could lead to contingencies such as life threatening emergencies and resulting search and rescue operations.[13] It is noteworthy that the U.S. Coast Guard has a limited capability to operate in the Arctic. With only three icebreakers—two of which are aging and not "in operational condition"[14]—demands could soon exceed its current capability by an unexpected growth in traffic in the Arctic. This could cause U.S. leaders to look to the Department of Defense to fill the capability gap that currently exists until other solutions are found.

Various observers have noted Arctic militarization activities as well. Rob Huebert points to the "rearming" of Arctic states,[15] and O'Rourke states that some see the Arctic "as a potential emerging security issue."[16] Both observers note that these issues are occurring concurrently with the ostensible ongoing cooperation.[17]

Included in the potential issues that the United States faces in the Arctic are difficulties in projecting force. The Department of Defense notes that a challenge for the U.S. is its "limited shore-based infrastructure" in the Arctic,[18] and other observers have perceived shortfalls in U.S.

---

[13] Department of Defense, *Report to Congress,* 11–12, 14, 29. The *Report to Congress* states that Search and Rescue "is a primary mission for the USCG" and "a secondary mission for the USN" (29).

[14] Ronald O'Rourke, *Coast Guard Polar Icebreaker Modernization: Background, Issues, and Options for Congress,* CRS Report for Congress (Washington D.C.: Congressional Research Service, 21 April 2011), 1.

[15] Rob Heubert, *The Newly Emerging Arctic Security Environment,* Canadian Defence and Foreign Affairs Institute, March 2010, http://www.cdfai.org/PDF/The%20Newly%20Emerging%20Arctic%20Security%20Environment.pdf (accessed September 12, 2011), 22.

[16] O'Rourke, *Changes in the Arctic,* Summary.

[17] Heubert, *Arctic Security Environment,* 4, 22; O'Rourke, *Changes in the Arctic,* Summary.

[18] Department of Defense, *Report to Congress,* 3.

infrastructure in the region.[19] This indicates that the lack of facilities to support a variety of contingencies may be one of the most important factors affecting operational risk.

This monograph investigates the hypothesis that increases in U.S. military responsibilities in geographic regions—with limited resources—lead to an increase in operational risk. The relevance of this hypothesis to a potential increase in responsibility for U.S. forces in the Arctic needs little explanation. Yet, for military leaders planning for the Arctic—in a period of fixed resources—the factors that most affect operational risk will be of the greatest interest. It is the thesis of this monograph that "facilities" is the most critical variable in addressing operational risk arising from a geo-environmental change. To that end, the questions that this monograph addresses are: (1) what historical cases can provide relevant information for U.S. geo-environmental change? and (2) what were the most important factors in those cases for addressing operational risk?

After a review of the relevant literature regarding the Arctic, as well as how the United States military deals with change, this monograph examines two historical case studies dealing with geo-environmental change. A case study on the Arctic follows. The final sections provide analysis, recommendations, and conclusions.

---

[19] Anthony L. Russell, "Carpe Diem: Seizing Strategic Opportunity in the Arctic," *Joint Forces Quarterly*, 51 (4th QTR 2008): 100. Russell recommends that "the United States should gradually establish the shore-based support infrastructure required for a near-continuous Arctic presence by 2020"; Conley and Kraut, *U.S. Strategic Interests*, 10. The authors state that, "The U.S. Navy and U.S. Coast Guard have recognized certain capability gaps that must be filled, chief among them search and rescue. The sudden and substantial increase in commercial shipping, marine tourism, and large passenger vessels in the Arctic poses significant challenges to the existing search-and-rescue infrastructure."

Chapter II: Literature Review

This literature review comprises two parts. First, it reviews works on the Arctic that identify its relevance to current security studies, as well as potential areas of concern to U.S. leaders. The second part identifies the key variables associated with historical geo-environmental changes to determine the most relevant variables with which to analyze the Arctic today.

The Arctic

A number of themes appear in the body of contemporary works on the Arctic. First, climate change is reducing ice levels, allowing increasing access to the region.[20] Second, there are vast and relatively untapped natural resources in the region—notably oil and natural gas.[21] This is understandably a source of interest to Arctic stakeholders and other interested parties. Conley and Kraut state that, "Access to oil, gas, minerals, fish, and transportation routes, formerly locked in by thick ice, are for the first time becoming accessible and viable sources of profit."[22]

Observers point to the potential increase in Arctic traffic that this could bring. Oran R. Young—a professor at the Bren School of Environmental Science and Management, University of California at Santa Barbara—states that, "The popular press focuses on the melting of sea ice and the prospect that this might unleash a rush to extract reserves of oil and gas" and other

---

[20] Theophilos Argitis, "Arctic Cabinet Meeting Risks New Cold War for Oil (Update1)," *Bloomberg,* 26 August 2008, http://www.bloomberg.com/apps/news?pid=21070001&sid=asUCKdhefIg4 (accessed 19 January 2012); Scott G. Borgerson, "Arctic Meltdown: The Economic and Security Implications of Global Warming," *Foreign Affairs,* March/April 2008, http://www.foreignaffairs.com/ articles/63222/scott-g-borgerson/arctic-meltdown (accessed 4 February 2012): 63; Ivar Kristiansen, "Arctic Frontiers: The Role of Pan-Arctic Bodies," *Conference of Parliamentarians of the Arctic Region,* 22 January 2007, http://www.arcticparl.org/files/images/speech%20Kristiansen%20Arctic%20Frontiers.pdf (accessed 12 January 2012), 3; O'Rourke, *Changes in the Arctic,* 1, 8.

[21] Borgerson, "Arctic Meltdown," 67; O'Rourke, *Changes in the Arctic,* 17–19. O'Rourke points to USGS estimates on petroleum.

[22] Conley and Kraut, *U.S. Strategic Interests,* 1.

activities.[23] Scott G. Borgerson warns that "the region could erupt in an armed mad dash for its resources."[24] For the U.S. military, as a global actor and an Arctic state (by virtue of Alaska), this represents a potential increase in responsibility.

Of further interest to the U.S. military is the potential increase in Arctic military activity—a source of concern for various Arctic stakeholders. Young has noted that media reporting can be overly dramatic regarding the Arctic and the possibilities for conflict there.[25] News stories with titles such as "Arctic Military Bases Signal New Cold War" and "US and Russia Stir up Political Tensions over Arctic" highlight some of the dramatic reactions to developments in the Arctic.[26] Yet, the Arctic states are cooperating,[27] and various commentators outside of the media tend to view the region through a relatively more analytical lens.[28] Young adds that "many reactions to this situation [Arctic changes] are more alarmist than alarming."[29] Reflecting the security ramifications for the Arctic states, national security professionals inside and outside of the United States have authored works on the Arctic, providing recommendations

---

[23] Oran R. Young, "The Arctic in Play: Governance in a Time of Rapid Change," *The International Journal of Marine and Coastal Law* 24 (2009): 426.

[24] Borgerson, "Arctic Meltdown," 65. Borgenson states that this is a possibility "without U.S. leadership to help develop diplomatic solutions to competing claims and potential conflicts."

[25] See, for example, Oran R. Young, "Whither the Arctic? Conflict or Cooperation in the Circumpolar North," *Polar Record* 45: 232 (2009): 74.

[26] Tim Reid, "Arctic Military Bases Signal New Cold War," *Times* [London, England] 11 August 2007: 39, *Academic OneFile,* Web, 11 February 2011; Terry Macalister, "US and Russia Stir Up Political Tensions Over Arctic," 6 July 2011, http://www.guardian.co.uk/world/2011/jul/06/us-russia-political-tensions-arctic (accessed 14 January 2012).

[27] Kristiansen, "Arctic Frontiers," 1.

[28] See, for example: Conley and Kraut, *U.S. Strategic Interests*; Russell, "Carpe Diem"; Kristiansen, "Arctic Frontiers."

[29] Young, "Whither the Arctic?," 73.

for their respective governments about how to address the region and its possibilities—both

positive and negative.[30]

Of the contemporary body of works on this topic, few have provided in-depth analysis of

historical cases to determine useful and applicable lessons for the Arctic in the future. For the

most part, contemporary analyses of the Arctic focus on current developments and their potential

ramifications. But, historical cases that could provide useful lessons do exist—and they are

relevant to the United States. This monograph considers a selection of those cases to inform the

current discourse on the Arctic. One of the most useful ways to help military planners frame the

environmental challenges[31] in the Arctic is an understanding of how the U.S. military has dealt

with geo-environmental changes in the past.

What are the key variables of geo-environmental change in the U.S. military?

Clearly, increased activity in the Arctic region represents a potential increase in

responsibilities for the U.S. military. This could require a reconfiguration within the U.S. military

to prevent an operational capability gap and its associated increase in operational risk. To assist in

this analysis, identifying key variables present during similar historical cases is helpful. But

which variables are the most relevant? The current U.S. doctrinal DOTMLPF framework —

---

[30] See, for example, Lieutenant Colonel Tarn M. Abell, "Arctic Security in a Warming World (Strategy Research Project, U.S. Army War College, 23 March 2010); Russell, "Carpe Diem"; Lieutenant Colonel Thomas R. McCarthy, Jr., "Global Warming Threatens National Interests in the Arctic" (Strategy Research Project, U.S. Army War College, 2009); Packard C. Trent, "An Evaluation of the Arctic—Will it Become an Area of Cooperation or Conflict?" (Thesis, Naval Postgraduate School, March 2011); MAJ Dave Abboud, "Safeguarding Canadian Arctic Sovereignty Against Conventional Threats" (Thesis, Command and General Staff School, 2009). For a non-military approach, see Chad P. Pate, "Easing the Arctic Tension: An Economic Solution" (Thesis, Naval Postgraduate School, December 2010).

[31] One of the three elements of the U.S. Army's Design method is "framing the operational environment." Department of the Army, *FM 5-0: The Operations Process* (Washington: Headquarters, Department of the Army, March 2010), 3-7.

doctrine, organization, training, materiel, leadership and education, personnel, and facilities[32]—offers a possibility. This is a tool available in the JCIDS (Joint Capabilities Integration and Development System) process to help inform military leaders about capability gaps.[33] But these variables apply with varying degrees of relevance to a U.S. military increase in responsibility in a geographic region. A more focused set of variables is indicated. Thus, this literature review will validate the most relevant variables to this monograph's subject area.

Doctrine and Organization

An increase in responsibility in a geographic region represents a significant environmental change—a geo-environmental change. A concept that approximates this type of change is the Revolution in Military Affairs (RMA), which might provide relevant insights into key variables. Williamson Murray and MacGregor Knox identify Doctrine, Organization, and Technology as key factors in RMAs: "Revolutions in military affairs require the assembly of a complex mix of tactical, organizational, doctrinal, and technological innovations in order to implement a new conceptual approach to warfare or to a specialized sub-branch of warfare."[34] This is reinforced by Clifford J. Rogers as well: "Commentators often view RMAs as driven above all by technology – but with the proviso that the development from innovation to revolution requires organizational and doctrinal adaptation before the tactical and strategic

---

[32] Department of Defense, *JP 1-02: Department of Defense Dictionary of Military and Associated Terms* ([Washington D.C.?]: 8 November 2010 (As Amended Through 15 August 2011)), A-46.

[33] Department of Defense, *CJCSI (Chairman of the Joint Chiefs of Staff Instruction) 3170.01G: Joint Capabilities Integration and Development System*, 1 March 2009, http://www.dtic.mil/cjcs_directives/cdata/unlimit/3170_01.pdf (accessed 11 September 2011), A-2. Although dated 1 March 2009, the document also states that it is "current as of 7 March 2011."

[34] Williamson Murray and MacGregor Knox, "Thinking about Revolutions in Warfare," in *The Dynamics of Military Revolution 1300–2050,* eds. MacGregor Knox and Williamson Murray (New York: Cambridge University Press, 2009). 12. Murray and Knox list "tactical" as well, but this monograph does not consider that variable in order to focus on the operational level of war.

potential of new weapon systems can be realized."[35] This highlights the importance of doctrine and organizational change in RMAs, and this study evaluates these changes in each case study; how the United States uses them to address operational risk in a geo-environmental change might be useful.

Technology

Technology has been seen as a driver in revolutions in military affairs.[36] This has been the case both inside and outside of the United States. Mark D. Mandeles states that, in the period following the American Civil War, "Many senior officers recognized the potential combat impact of new weapons technologies, such as the flat trajectory magazine rifle, high explosives, smokeless power, and quick-firing artillery," although there was "disagreement" about the implications of these innovations for the U.S. military.[37] He further states that, "Understanding the implications of new weapons technologies required recognizing the new capabilities as different from current capabilities and then designing or devising appropriate organizations, doctrine, and training to adapt."[38] Williamson Murray and Allan R. Millett reinforce Mandeles's statements on technology when they include "the rapid pace of technological change" in the "factors [that] have driven innovation in military affairs."[39] This monograph, however, hypothesizes that an increase in responsibility in a geographic region can drive change instead of a technological or other driver. Yet, as technology can be seen as an integral part of historical military changes, its effect on operational risk is also relevant here.

---

[35] Rogers, "New Sun," in Knox and Murray, 18.

[36] Ibid.

[37] Mark D. Mandeles, *Military Transformation Past and Present: Historical Lessons for the 21st Century* (Connecticut: Praeger Security International, 2007), 15.

[38] Ibid., 19.

[39] Williamson Murray and Allan R. Millett, introduction to *Military Innovation in the Interwar Period,* eds. Williamson Murray and Allan R. Millett (New York: Cambridge University Press, 2009), 1.

10

Facilities

"Facilities" is the final element in the DOTMLPF framework. This is a critical variable for evaluating potential operational risk resulting from increases in responsibility in a geographic region—especially one distant from U.S. shores. Increases in responsibilities in geographic regions suggest a requirement to project force in an expeditionary manner. This requires bases and facilities. However, the United States has infrastructure in place around the globe today. The question will be whether the facilities in place are sufficient to mitigate the potential operational risk resulting from these geo-environmental changes. And, if the U.S. military, given limited resources, has the ability to mitigate operational risk through adequate facilities.

Threat

In a region of increased responsibilities, real or potential threats will affect operational risk. This has been the case since the early years of the United States. Mandeles notes that, "The frontier war against the Indians shaped post-Civil War thought about force structure, tactics, training, and acquisition in ways that were inappropriate for combat against European adversaries."[40]

In a relevant example for this monograph, the United States realized a perceived requirement to project force abroad in 1898 when the United States acquired the Philippines. The emergence of Japan as a strong power[41] presented an operational threat in the Asia-Pacific region.

---

[40] Mandeles, *Military Transformation*, 15.

[41] Mandeles notes that Article XIX of the 1922 Naval Limitation Treaty "formalized Japan's world lead in amphibious forces, doctrine, and technology ... and enhanced the U.S. requirement for an amphibious assault capability in a conflict with Japan." Ibid., 50. In a note, Mandeles also points to Henry Steele Commager, ed., *Documents of American History*, 8th ed. (New York: Appleton-Century-Crofts, 1968), 181–183; Edward S. Miller, *War Plan Orange: The U.S. Strategy to Defeat Japan, 1897–1945* (Annapolis, MD: Naval Institute Press, 1991), 75; Allan R. Millett, "Assault from the Sea, the Development of Amphibious Assault between the Wars," in *Innovation in the Interwar Period,* eds. Allan

11

Major Earl Ellis, author of Operations Plan 712, *Advanced Base Force Operations in Micronesia*, stated that, "In order to impose our will upon Japan, it will be necessary for us to project our fleet and land forces across the Pacific and wage war in Japanese waters. To effect this requires that we have sufficient bases to support the fleet, both during its projecting and afterward."[42] These factors indicate the importance of measuring the relative threat level in this monograph's case studies.

Analysis

A review of works on U.S. military change illustrates a few themes. First, a number of works on RMAs indicate the importance of changes in Doctrine, Organization, Technology, and other factors. Second, there is a relative paucity of coverage on drivers of change and related variables for increases in responsibilities in geographic regions.[43] If technology has been a key historical driver in RMAs, what happens when the driver for change comes not from technology or other typical factors—but from a geo-environmental change? Also, although other elements in the DOTMLPF construct are discussed to varying degrees in these works, their importance relative to the DOT variables in a geo-environmental change appears negligible—with the

---

R. Millet and Williamson Murray (Washington DC: OSD/NA, June 1994), 68; Holland M. Smith and Percy Finch, *Coral and Brass* (New York: Ace Books, 1949), 73.

[42] As cited in Mandeles, *Military Transformation,* 61.

[43] The coverage is not non-existent, however. For example, in 2008, Dennis R. Penn, a student at the U.S. Army War College, investigated what he asserted was a Revolution in Military Affairs regarding a "proactive peacetime engagement as a way to achieving national strategy objectives" in regard to USAFRICOM and U.S military engagement in Africa. Dennis R. Penn, "Africa Command and the Militarization of U.S. Foreign Policy," Strategy Research Project (Carlisle Barracks, U.S. Army War College, 2008), 7. In another example, in 2001, Robert D. Gibson, a student at the U.S. Army War College, stated that "space has matured into an essential venue for military operations," and asserts that "Space power is the true revolution in military affairs." Robert D. Gibson, "Space Power, *The* Revolution in Military Affairs" (Carlisle: U.S. Army War College, 2001), iii. Although space may be a domain, rather than a geographic region, an increase in U.S. military responsibilities in space is analogous in that it represents an environmental change for the U.S. military.

exception of facilities. Selecting an existing analytical framework (such as DOTMLPF) may then be insufficient to effectively analyze a geo-environmental change.

These factors suggest that the Doctrine, Organization, and Technology variables alone are insufficient for this examination, and the DOTMLPF framework covers more than is needed for a focused discussion. As integral to RMAs, the Doctrine, Organization, and Technology factors will serve as the start point. "Facilities" is added from the DOTMLPF elements, and "threat" serves as the final variable. The variables used in this work are then: (1) Doctrine, (2) Organization, (3) Technology, (4) Facilities, and (5) Threat—or DOTTF. Thus, the key RMA variables are combined with threat and the most relevant of the DOTMLPF variables. This framework attempts to provide two things: (1) a relevant and structured analytical framework to inform an "ill-structured problem"[44] in the Arctic region, and (2) it chooses a qualitative rather than a quantitative method to analyze a problem fraught with the uncertainties of geo-politics and the future of the Arctic.

---

[44] The U.S. Army uses the term "ill-structured problems" within the context of Design in current doctrine. U.S. Army doctrine describes an ill-structured problem as a "task unfamiliar" to those facing it. Department of the Army, *FM 5-0*, 3-2, 3-3. The description is on page 3-3.

13

Chapter III: Methodology

This monograph investigates the hypothesis that increases in U.S. military responsibilities in geographic regions (with limited resources) lead to an increase in operational risk. An increase in responsibility will lead to a real or perceived requirement to construct a campaign plan in response. These plans are evident in the historical cases examined here.

This monograph analyzes these cases through a number of variables. The independent variables are increases in responsibilities in geographic regions. The intervening variables are: Doctrine, Organization, Technology, Threat, and Facilities (DOTTF). The dependent variable is operational risk for U.S. forces. Given an increase in responsibility in a geographic region, this monograph analyzes how the United States, given a limited pool of resources, historically addressed the five variables in light of the geo-environmental change. This paper measures the variables individually by examining their effect on operational risk—did they cause operational risk to go up or down? The change in the dependent variable (operational risk) is then viewed by gauging the overall effect of the five variables on operational risk for the case.

This monograph defines operational risk in accordance with the Department of Defense's Joint Publication 1-02, where it defines risk as the "probability and severity of loss linked to hazards."[45] In this case, operational risk is the likelihood of an event or outcome in a geographic region that prevents the U.S. military from achieving its strategic objectives. According to U.S. Army doctrine, "Inadequate planning and preparation recklessly risks forces."[46] This otherwise obvious statement indicates the importance of planning and preparing in the wake of geo-

---

[45] Department of Defense, *JP 1-02,* 297.

[46] Department of the Army, *FM 3-0: Operations (with Change 1)* (Washington D.C.: Headquarters, Department of the Army, February 2008 (Change 1: 22 February 2011)), 7-15.

environmental changes. Central to this work is how the United States has and can mitigate operational risk incurred by geo-environmental change through management of key variables.

The case studies chosen feature the U.S. military, occur for the most part after 1900, and focus on areas dominated by seas, oceans, and littorals. The first historical case study scrutinizes the increase in U.S. military responsibilities in the Asia–Pacific region after the United States acquired the Philippines in 1898. The second case study examines the increase in U.S. military responsibilities in the Indian Ocean region after the British announced their intention to retrench from their colonial empire in the "East of Suez"[47] area. This monograph then applies the knowledge gained from these case studies to the Arctic region.

A variety of additional historical case studies are available to inform a discussion about an increase in responsibilities in the Arctic region. Some are relevant, such as the increase in U.S. responsibilities (or at least the perception of such) in outer space after the launch of Sputnik in 1957. However, in the interest of space, it is useful to focus the discussion on the United States military, although the 2010 Quadrennial Defense Review notes the importance of U.S. Government Interagency collaboration in the Arctic.[48] Likewise, in an effort to retain relevancy, this monograph does not consider cases of geo-environmental changes prior to the twentieth century, such as the new possibilities offered in the Asia–Pacific region after Commodore Perry's actions in Japan in 1854. Finally, land-based cases, such as the increase in U.S. military

---

[47] Various works feature the "East of Suez" concept. For example, according to Monoranjan Bezboruah, British Prime Minister Harold Wilson stated, "Great Britain could not afford to relinquish its world role—a role, which, 'for shorthand purposes, is sometimes called our "east of Suez" role.'" As cited in Monoranjan Bezboruah, *U.S. Strategy in the Indian Ocean: The International Response* (Praeger: New York, 1977), 20. For another example, see Saki Dockrill's 2002 book on this region: Saki Dockrill, *Britain's Retreat from East of Suez: The Choice between Europe and the World?* (Houndmills, Basingstoke, Hampshire: Palgrave MacMillan, 2002).

[48] Department of Defense, *Report to Congress*, 8.

responsibilities in central and western Europe after World War II, are less relevant to this

discussion due to the water-dominated environment of the Arctic.

Chapter IV: Case studies

The following two historical cases studies each outline the history, strategic context, and other relevant information that might help inform operational planners in geo-environmental changes. The case studies then examine operational risk through the DOTTF variables to identify which are the most critical in addressing this change. An analysis section concludes each case study.

The Asia–Pacific region after the Spanish–American War

This case study examines the effect on operational risk from an increase in U.S. responsibility for U.S. forces in the Asia–Pacific region after the U.S. acquisition of the Philippines in 1898. The case study ends at the beginning of the Washington Conference in 1921.

In the aftermath of the Spanish–American War, the Philippines passed from Spain to the United States. U.S. military interest in the Asia–Pacific region began growing soon after.[49] Although the United States was no stranger to the Far East, the Philippines represented a significant foothold for the United States in this region. Before this, the United States had not maintained a significant, sustained military presence. Stanley B. Weeks and Charles A. Meconis state that, "In early 1898 only a small squadron of second-rate US naval vessels patrolled the Western Pacific, and there were no American ground troops there. This minimal military presence matched the lack of commitment to the region at that time."[50] By 1902, when the

---

[49] It is worthwhile to note that Weeks and Meconis state, "The commitment of significant US forces in the Philippines and China from 1898 to 1902 did have lasting consequences, but it did not lead immediately to a major commitment to the region." Stanley B. Weeks and Charles A. Meconis, *The Armed Forces of the USA in the Asia–Pacific Region* (New York: I.B. Taurus, 1999), 10. As discussed in the case study, increases in U.S. engagement in the region took place over decades.

[50] Weeks and Meconis, *Armed Forces*, 8.

conflict between U.S. forces and Filipino fighters (the Philippine–American War) had officially ended,[51] the increase in U.S. responsibilities in the region was evident.

Besides responsibilities, the political decision to secure the Philippines from Spain also generated strategic possibilities for the United States. In the case of conflict in the Far East, "With a Philippine base, the United States might be able to fight a short and victorious war; without one it would have to mount a long and costly campaign across the Pacific," according to Brian McAllister Linn.[52] But these possibilities came with a price. Linn tells us that, as early as 1899, "it had become clear that America's newly won empire entailed considerable expense."[53]

The U.S. Army's involvement in the Philippines after 1898 suggested changes ahead for the War Department. Soldiers might now be drawn on to protect America's budding empire—a previously unpracticed role. According to Linn, "for the army the defense of the overseas possessions required a substantial recasting of traditional military ideas," and the "overseas garrison's primary task was to protect naval bases and thus insure the U.S. Navy's ability to move its fleet throughout the Pacific, a subsidiary role quite the opposite of its independence in continental coast defense."[54]

Although U.S. Army forces were required to end the conflict during the Philippine–American War, the distances between the Asia–Pacific region and the continental United States indicated a relatively prominent role for the U.S. Navy in the years ahead. William Reynolds Braisted relates the following finding from a War Department Board of Review in 1915: "Hard

---

[51] Weeks and Meconis, *Armed Forces*, 10. Weeks and Meconis also point to the following source: John M. Gates, "The Pacification of the Philippines," in *The American Military and the Far East,* ed. Joe C. Dixon (Washington D.C.: US Government Printing Office, 1980), 79–91.

[52] Brian McAllister Linn, *Guardians of Empire: The U.S. Army and the Pacific, 1902–1940* (Chapel Hill: University of North Carolina Press, 1997), 82.

[53] Ibid., 11.

[54] Ibid., 80. Linn discusses this idea on pages 79–80.

pressed to find a mission in the Philippines, the Board of Review resolved to approach the Navy, since the islands' relation to national defense was 'in its broader aspects, *a naval rather than a military question.*'"[55] The primacy of sea power seems self-evident in evaluating operational risks related to the Philippines; but, with the benefit of hindsight, a War Department diagnosis assigning the Navy as the sole interested party seems somewhat shortsighted. Nevertheless, in the waking hours of the twentieth century, the Department of the Navy must have seemed an obvious direction in which to turn to address the strategic relevance of the Philippines and the Asia–Pacific region.

Operations in the region would also cause the Department of the Navy to change its ways of thinking and operating. According to Braisted, the Spanish–American War "brought in its wake a stream of consequences which converted the Navy from a Western Hemisphere defense force to the protector of an empire extending halfway around the world."[56] He further notes that, "The war forced American naval men for the first time to plan simultaneous operations on opposite sides of the globe."[57] The United States' new territories—Guam, Hawaii, and the Philippines—"formed the western anchors of a life line of naval empire that would extend from the Atlantic Coast westward by an isthmian canal to Asia."[58]

For U.S. political leaders, military considerations were not the only concern. American economic interests in the region were also at stake. In the early years of the twentieth century, "US economic interests in the region continued to grow," according to Weeks and Meconis (even

---

[55] As cited in William Reynolds Braisted, *The United States Navy in the Pacific, 1909–1922* (Austin: University of Texas, 1971), 249. Italics mine.

[56] William Reynolds Braisted, *The United States Navy in the Pacific, 1897–1909* (New York: Greenwood Press, 1969), 21.

[57] Braisted, *Navy in the Pacific, 1909–1922*, 4.

[58] Ibid.

though "Europe remained preeminent as an American trade partner").[59] By 1902, exports to the

Far East had increased compared to just a few years before.[60] In 1906, Wolf von Schierbrand

pointed to a role for the military in protecting commercial shipping in the region when he noted

that the relatively large size of British maritime forces compared to U.S. maritime forces "is too

much to our disadvantage if we seriously contemplate commercial, and *its absolutely necessary*

correlate, naval, preponderance in the Pacific."[61]

The post-Philippine–American War period

Weeks and Meconis indicate that, beginning in 1907, U.S. commitment to the region took

a downward turn.[62] They provide four reasons for the "lack of a major US military commitment

to the Asia–Pacific region" over the following decades: (1) the region's secondary status to

Europe as a trade partner, (2) the lack of a credible threat to U.S. forces, (3) the fact that "no

bureaucratic commitments to East Asia emerged either in the State Department or the military,"

and (4) "the rapid decline of interest among the American public once most US troops had left the

Philippines and the rebellion had quietened down."[63] Weeks and Meconis assert that "these four

factors … shaped the declining American presence for 30 years."[64]

---

[59] Weeks and Meconis, *Armed Forces*, 11.

[60] George Hamlin Fitch, "The New Pacific Empire," *The World's Work III*, (November 1901–April 1902). 1592. Fitch stated, "To meet the remarkable growth of the export trade there has been a correspondingly large and sudden increase in shipping facilities." He gives the following figures: "The official figures of exports from Pacific Coast ports show a total in 1890 of 44 ½ million dollars' worth; in 1896, 59 million; in 1898, 62 ½ million; in 1900, 73 ⅓ million." Wolf Von Schierbrand noted "a recent annual report of the San Francisco Chamber of Commerce" which stated, "We sold Asia $43,000,000 worth of goods in 1902, against $15,000,000 in 1892": Wolf Von Schierbrand, "The Coming Supremacy of the Pacific: Sixth Paper—The Need of a Large Navy," *The Pacific Monthly*, January 1906, 100–101. It is not clear if both authors are considering the same set of import countries; however, both indicate a similar increase in export activity.

[61] Von Schierbrand, "Coming Supremacy," 98–99. Italics mine.

[62] Weeks and Meconis, *Armed Forces*, 10–11.

[63] Ibid., 11. In a note, Weeks and Meconis point to the following sources: Roger Dingman, "American Policy and Strategy in East Asia 1898–1950: The Creation of a Commitment," in *The American*

Lack of interest from the American public regarding the Asia–Pacific region seemed to influence the views of politicians on the area—with operational ramifications for the U.S. military in the region. Braisted states that, "Roosevelt confided to Taft in August, 1907, that he believed the Philippines had become the American 'heel of Achilles.' Since the American people were unwilling to support fortifications or a navy adequate to defend the islands, Roosevelt favored giving them independence before the United States was forced out under duress."[65] Braisted also notes that, between 1909 and 1922, the Navy did not "win national support for its plan to project its power across the Pacific by building bases west of Pearl Harbor."[66]

For an operational planner, a lack of clear policy and strategic direction is concerning. Yet, planners in 1912–1914 certainly had to deal with this challenge. According to Braisted, "The foremost political factor influencing military thought on the Philippines was the uncertainty regarding the future of the United States in the islands."[67] He further relates that, "When the War Department tried to frame a Philippine program in response to the preparedness movement in 1915, it was again plagued by uncertainty regarding the islands' future status."[68]

In 1916, the military obtained some strategic direction. President Wilson "directed that, in case of war in the Far East, the joint mission of military and naval forces in the Philippines would be: *'To defend Manila and Manila Bay.'*"[69] This guidance helped military leaders make

---

Military and the Far East, ed. Joe C. Dixon (Washington DC: U.S. Government Printing Office, 1980), 25–27.

[64] Weeks and Meconis, *Armed Forces,* 11.

[65] Braisted, *Navy in the Pacific, 1897–1909,* 216.

[66] Braisted, *Navy in the Pacific, 1909–1922,* viii.

[67] Ibid., 246.

[68] Ibid., 250.

[69] As cited in Braisted, *Navy in the Pacific, 1909–1922,* 252. Italics in original. Braisted also points to the following source: William M. Ingraham to Secretary of the Navy, 10 October 1916, in Secretary of the Navy's General Records, No. 11406-756, NA, RG 80,

operational DOTMLPF decisions in the Asia–Pacific region in the coming years.[70] It also gave

operational planners significant leeway in deciding how best to support the strategic objective.

Post-WWI

After World War I, military planners for the Asia–Pacific region faced a challenge that

continues to echo today—how to mitigate operational risk and prepare for the future with limited

or even declining resources. In the post-WWI era, among many possible paths, there was no

clear, best answer. Further complicating matters, planners labored under the cloud of unclear

strategic objectives. According to Braisted, in 1919, the Joint Board considered bases "at Hawaii,

Guam, and the Philippines"—which would require additional preparations at Guam—as

important to defeating Japan militarily in a war in the western Pacific.[71] However, the members of

the Joint Board were concerned that "the proposed Guam base touched doubtful areas of foreign

policy," and considered that, "If the United States intended only to keep Japan out of the eastern

Pacific, there was no need for a base farther west than Pearl Harbor."[72] The Joint Board was

seeking strategic guidance which would not immediately come.[73] Undoubtedly military leaders

knew that clear strategic objectives—or the lack of them—in this area would shape operational

DOTMLPF decisions with long-term ramifications.

---

[70] Braisted states that, "Adoption of this mission paved the way for new gestures toward closing the naval station at Subic Bay. Admiral Winterhalter and the joint defense board in the Philippines were convinced that the naval utilities at Olongapo should be shifted to behind the defenses at Manila Bay." Braisted, *Navy in the Pacific, 1909–1922*, 252. Braisted also points to the following source: Report by Joint Army and Navy Board, Manila, 15 November 1916, memoranda by naval members, 14 November 1916, Secretary of the Navy's General Records, No. 11406/603, NA, RG 80. Braisted also states that Secretary of the Navy Daniels "announced in December 1916 the 'eventual removal' of the naval station from Olongapo to Cavite." As cited in Braisted, *Navy in the Pacific, 1909–1922*, 252–253. Braisted also points to the following source: Daniels to Naval Station, Olongapo, 19 December 1916, Secretary of the Navy's General Records, No. 27403/503. NA, RG. 80.

[71] Braisted, *Navy in the Pacific, 1909–1922*, 474–475.

[72] Ibid., 475.

[73] Ibid., 475–476. See also Braisted's chapter, "Struggle for a Pacific Policy, 1920," beginning on page 477.

The Washington Conference, beginning in 1921, would bring additional political and strategic guidance for military leaders and planners, although it may not have made their ability to prepare easier. This agreement between the United States, Great Britain, and Japan, "had [a] lasting impact on Pacific strategy."[74] According to Weeks and Meconis, it "included a ratio of 5:5:3 for the major warships of those three countries [respectively], major reductions in naval tonnage, and a ban on further development of bases and fortifications in the Pacific, including the Philippines."[75] Weeks and Meconis conclude that, "Its immediate impact was to hasten the decline of an American presence in the Pacific."[76] This decline would not begin reversing until 1938.[77] By then, however, the major operational decisions that would affect U.S. interests in the region for the duration of World War II—notably facilities choices and the organization and materials that would be available in case of conflict—had been made. Even if military planners had foreseen the Japanese attacks on U.S. possessions in the Pacific in the early 1940s, major shifts in operational planning and preparations would have been challenging. This highlights the importance of operational planners making effective long-term choices to achieve political objectives in strategic regions—as well as the presence of clear political objectives to help guide those choices.

In some cases, the planning decisions made would not be sufficient to prevent American setbacks in the Asia–Pacific region in the coming years. Brian McAllister Linn states that his 1997 book, *Guardians of Empire: The U.S. Army and the Pacific, 1902–1940*, is partly "a study of how modern military institutions, staffed by intelligent and committed professionals, can work devotedly, and generate sophisticated projects and plans, but still not address the central issues

---

[74] Weeks and Meconis, *Armed Forces*, 11.
[75] Ibid., 11–12.
[76] Ibid., 12.
[77] Ibid.

23

that confront them."[78] Linn's statement is a frank analysis of a challenging period for U.S. operational planners who made long-term decisions spanning the DOTMLPF spectrum, and apparently missed the mark—at least in part. To see what Linn is referring to, an examination of the key considerations during the period is useful.

Key variables analysis

Doctrine

Across the U.S. military, there was a shift in how it would do business after 1898. For example, of the years following the Philippine–American War of 1898–1902, Linn states, "In the Pacific possessions, as in the continental United States, the army's mission was to fortify and defend strategic harbors; but beyond this similarity, continental and overseas defense displayed numerous differences."[79] The Navy as well had to determine how to deal with a possession far from the shores of the continental United States. Thus, the U.S. military began a shift from a focus on continental defense to a more expeditionary way of thinking. Yet, although the U.S. Army had to assume a constabulary function,[80] the geo-environmental change did not generate a sweeping change in Army doctrine.[81] It is difficult to say whether this status quo contributed to American losses in the region in the 1940s. Doctrine's affect on operational risk is undetermined.

---

[78] Linn, *Guardians of Empire*, xiv. Linn is apparently referring to U.S. Army planners.

[79] Ibid., 79.

[80] Ibid., 24–27.

[81] Walter E. Kretchik, *U.S. Army Doctrine: From the American Revolution to the War on Terror* (Lawrence, Kansas: University Press of Kansas, 2011), 104. Kretchik states that, "From 1898 through the early 1900s, the Army learned valuable lessons from its military governance and multinational experiences in the Caribbean and Asia. Still, no effort was made to significantly alter army doctrine to accommodate that knowledge."

Organization

The organization of the U.S. military was affected by the U.S. acquisitions in the Asia–Pacific region. The Army was no exception. The quantity and disposition of Army forces in the region was a key question. Although about 125,000 soldiers were employed during the Philippine–American War,[82] the "Philippine Constabulary" numbered about 7,500 soon after the conflict was over.[83] Secretary of War Taft described the entire U.S. Army of 1902–1914 as "nothing but a skeleton army,"[84] providing some insight as to the amount of forces that could be employed across the Pacific Ocean. Braisted referred to "the Army's regiments in the Philippines" as "suicide forces, which at best could keep the flag flying on Corregidor and the little islands at the entrances to Manila and Subic Bays during war with Japan."[85] Linn summarizes these challenges with the statement that, "Certainly in the case of the Pacific Army, the nation's declared policy to defend the overseas territories was confounded by a dearth of resources to do it."[86]

The Navy had similar resource challenges. In the period just after the Philippine–American War, one of its "three major objectives" in the region was "the establishment of an Asiatic Fleet including a division of battleships capable of competing with the other fleets in the

---

[82] Linn, *Guardians of Empire*, 15.

[83] Ibid., 24. Linn also points to H. W. Brands, *Bound to Empire: The United States and the Philipppines* (New York: Oxford University Press, 1992), 60–79; Karnow, *In Our Image: America's Empire in the Philippines* (New York: Random House, 1989), 196–211; Garel A. Grunder and William E. Livezey, *The Philippines and the United States* (Norman: University of Oklahoma Press, 1951), 78–145.

[84] Testimony of William H. Taft, U.S. Congress, Senate, Committee on Military Affairs, *Hearings before the Committee of Military Affairs (Senate), on the Army Appropriations Act, 1906–7,* (Washington D.C.: Government Printing Office, 1906), 39, quoted in Linn, *Guardians of Empire*, 55.

[85] Braisted, *Navy in the Pacific, 1909–1922*, 61. Braisted does not note specific dates, but this passage is couched within his book section that covers "The Taft Years, 1909–1913."

[86] Linn, *Guardians of Empire*, xiv. Linn is apparently discussing the period 1902–1940, the scope of his book.

area" (although a 1903 decision shifted the concentration of battleships to the Atlantic).[87]

According to Braisted, the Navy's General Board was aiming for "forty-eight battleships and

twenty-four armored cruisers" Navy-wide by 1919.[88] But constraints from Washington—between

President Roosevelt and authorizations from Congress—seemed likely to limit the Navy's desired

fleet endstate.[89]

Other factors influenced the resources that the United States Navy could apply in the

Asia–Pacific region. U.S. national interests in the Atlantic still outweighed Pacific concerns. In

1901–1904, "Although the United States attempted to station battleships in the Pacific as well as

in the Atlantic, its heavy units in the latter outnumbered those in the former by two to one,"

according to Braisted.[90] The Navy gradually made changes to its organization to support its new

responsibilities in the western Pacific. Weeks and Meconis relate that, "In 1907 the US Navy

established a Pacific Fleet, although all US battleships were stationed in the Atlantic, and in 1910

the Asiatic Squadron was upgraded to become the Asiatic Fleet."[91] Yet, the Atlantic–Pacific

balance decision was important enough that organizational planners would take their strategic

direction from the very top. Braisted relates that, in 1908, President Roosevelt "remained

convinced that the battleships should not be divided."[92] This meant that the heavy punch of the

U.S. battleships would remain in the Atlantic for the time being. Finally, the Navy had to

determine how best to stretch its material assets. To supply U.S. forces in the Asia–Pacific region

---

[87] Braisted, *Navy in the Pacific, 1909–1922*, 5–6. The other two objectives were "the construction of a war base at Subic Bay in the Philippines, and the acquisition of an advanced base on the China Coast, preferably in the Chusan Archipelago or in Fukien" (5).

[88] Braisted, *Navy in the Pacific, 1897–1909*, 173.

[89] Ibid.; Braisted, *Navy in the Pacific, 1909–1922*, 65.

[90] Braisted, *Navy in the Pacific, 1897–1909*, 115–116. The quoted passage is on 116.

[91] Weeks and Meconis, *Armed Forces*, 10.

[92] Braisted, *Navy in the Pacific, 1897–1909*, 225. In a note, Braisted points to the following source: Bell to Taft, 7 February 1908, with endorsement by Roosevelt, Wood to Roosevelt, 30 January 1908, Roosevelt Papers.

required not only facilities and clear lines of communication, but also vessels to transport men and materials. Braisted states that, "To supply the fleet with coal and other material necessary for operations distant from its home ports, the Navy would require, in the [Naval War] college's estimate, some one hundred ships aggregating over 500,000 tons, in addition to shipping available from domestic sources."[93]

These examples highlight the challenges that operational planners can encounter while trying to meet strategic objectives with limited and/or declining resources. Protection of U.S. interests in the Asia–Pacific region was ostensibly important to U.S. political leaders, but declining interest in the region constrained the manner in which military planners could pursue those goals. Finally, fiscal and political limitations caused the organization levels to fall short of that desired by U.S. military leaders in the region. Together, these various organizational challenges translated to an increase in operational risk for U.S. planners and leaders.

Technology

U.S. leaders pursued technological improvements in this period that had implications for Asia–Pacific operations. One technological change was the shift from coal to oil in U.S. naval vessels. The United States introduced the first oil-burning U.S. naval ship in 1910 and continued the shift in the following years.[94] This technological change to oil offered a greater range for the U.S. fleet,[95] which had ramifications for military forces in the Asia–Pacific region.

---

[93] Braisted, *Navy in the Pacific, 1909–1922*, 34. Braisted notes that the War College's thoughts stem from "its studies for the Orange Plan."

[94] Erik J. Dahl, "Naval Innovation: From Coal to Oil," *Joint Forces Quarterly* (Winter 2000–2001), 54.

[95] Ibid., 51.

Other relevant technological changes also centered around the Navy. Theodore Roosevelt worked to address his perception of "gaps" in U.S. naval capabilities.[96] The drivers for his pursuance of "new technology" to fill these gaps included "an inability to operate at great distances from U.S.-controlled shore bases" as well as limitations on the U.S.'s ability to go "toe-to-toe with certain foreign navies."[97] To deal with these issues, Roosevelt "sought to change the very design and capabilities of the ships under his command"[98] in order to create a fleet that would be "equal to or better than any contemporary design in the world."[99] Roosevelt was heavily engaged in fleet modernization, from detailed discussions about the caliber of weapons on the U.S. Navy's *New Hampshire* to broader topics such as "the selection of a new gun sight for the fleet's large-caliber weapons."[100] In the end, Roosevelt had created "a modern Navy arrayed around a strategic centerpiece, the all-big-gun battleship."[101] Even though the technological improvements were apparently not directly aimed at operations in the Asia–Pacific region, the qualitative improvements in the U.S. Navy's vessels may have reduced operational risk to some degree there. Given American losses in the 1940s, it seems that the reduction was not sufficient.

The Threat

Existing or potential threats can play a significant part in generating operational risk after a geo-environmental change. For the Asia–Pacific region in the early twentieth century, the threat was clear to U.S. leaders and planners—Japan. According to Braisted, "In 1909 no problem in the

---

[96] Henry J. Hendrix, *Theodore Roosevelt's Naval Diplomacy: The U.S. Navy and the Birth of the American Century* (Annapolis: Naval Institute Press: 2009), 132.

[97] Ibid., 132.

[98] Ibid., 133.

[99] Ibid., 134.

[100] Ibid., 140, 142. The quoted text is from page 140.

[101] Ibid., 154. In a note, Hendrix points to the following source: Matthew M. Oyos, "Theodore Roosevelt and the Implements of War," *Journal of Military History* 60, No. 4 (1996): 634.

Pacific puzzled American strategists more than the defense of the Philippines. The islands had been suddenly transformed into the weakest element in the entire American defense system as Japan emerged a possible enemy of really formidable power after 1906."[102]

The Japanese threat to the Philippines was not lost on America's senior civilian leaders. Braisted tells us that, in 1906, a memorandum was prepared "At Roosevelt's request … which stressed that the United States was helpless to stem a Japanese attack before the Philippines, Hawaii, and even the Pacific coast states were overrun."[103] The Army shared these concerns, and "Roosevelt received the most urgent appeals from army officers who recognized their total inability to defend American territories adequately in the Pacific with the limited forces at their command."[104] The Navy understood as well what was at stake: "West of Pearl Harbor … the Navy's outlook was extremely uncertain during the four years after 1909. Naval men were under obligation to defend the Philippines and to win control of the western Pacific should Japan attack."[105]

For U.S. military planners—in the face of their increase in responsibility—this threat translated to an increase in operational risk. The problem was how to defend America's western Pacific possessions against potential aggression from Japan. It is true that there was a "rough sketch for war against Japan, known as the Orange Plan,"[106] which evolved into a "first draft" by 1914.[107] But there was more work to be done in the years ahead to address operational risk within the strategic framework provided in the Asia–Pacific region.

---

[102] Braisted, *Navy in the Pacific, 1909–1922*, 59.

[103] Braisted, *Navy in the Pacific, 1897–1909*, 192.

[104] Ibid., 225.

[105] Braisted, *Navy in the Pacific, 1909–1922*, 58.

[106] Ibid., 31.

[107] Weeks and Meconis, *Armed Forces*, 11.

Facilities

Facilities concerns may have been the most critical aspect of developing operational plans for the Asia–Pacific region following the Philippines War. A primary concern for naval planners was creating a clear line of communication between the western coast of the United States and the new American possessions. Braisted notes that, as early as 1898–1899, it was important for the Navy to construct "a protected line of communications" between the Western Atlantic and the Western Pacific.[108] In light of the threat from Japan, the Navy's ability to move combat power to the Asia–Pacific region to protect U.S. interests relied on the "construction of a chain of protected bases along a communications line that extended from the Atlantic, through a fortified isthmian canal to the Pacific, and across the Pacific to the Philippines."[109] Yet, military planners had a variety of possibilities for bases and facilities. And ill-considered decisions could have long-term ramifications for American interests in this area of the world.

Basing decisions are critical—not least because of their cost and enduring nature—and the Pacific was no exception. U.S. forces would require them to extend their operational reach across the Pacific. According to Braisted, "Ultimate American victory would depend on whether the United States could dispatch and support its battle fleet in enemy waters more than ten thousand miles from its starting point in the Atlantic. The project involved logistic problems of previously unimagined magnitude."[110]

But which locations would best support America's future operational plans in support of strategic goals? Although the Navy considered "an advanced base in China,"[111] building the links

---

[108] Braisted, *Navy in the Pacific, 1897–1909*, 63.

[109] Braisted, *Navy in the Pacific, 1909–1922*, viii.

[110] Ibid., 31.

[111] Braisted, *Navy in the Pacific, 1897–1909*, 116.

in the lines of communication would require stops that spanned the vast area of the Pacific. The United States gained the eastern islands of Samoa on 2 December 1899[112]—which Secretary of State John Hay considered a key Pacific harbor[113]—but Braisted notes that Captain Crowninshield from the Bureau of Navigation "had correctly predicted that Pago Pago, being far removed from the Navy's main lines of communication, would have little significance as a naval position."[114] Hawaii was another important possibility. In 1898, American "annexationists" made the case "that it was necessary for the successful prosecution of military operations in the Philippines."[115] In 1901, a War Department committee affirmed the importance of Pearl Harbor and stated that, "Without it, the defense of the Philippines was impossible," according to Linn.[116]

Fairly early, the possible locations for U.S. bases were settled. Braisted states that, "With the partition of Samoa [in 1899], the United States had obtained the principal territories that constituted her overseas domain in the Pacific for the next forty years."[117] Whether they knew it or not, the framework that military planners had to work with in the Asia–Pacific region was in place. Yet, this framework provided a range of options. The choice of how to array the bases that would sustain forces—and the ports that would facilitate shipping—in the western Pacific was also critical.

For the Navy, the lack of ports was concerning. In the first decade of the twentieth century, according to Braisted, "Of far more serious consequence to the United States than the actual number of ships immediately available was the total absence of a war base in the

---

[112] Braisted, *Navy in the Pacific, 1897–1909*, 62.

[113] As cited in Braisted, *Navy in the Pacific, 1897–1909*, 62–63. Braisted quotes the following source: Hay to Choate, 4 December 1899, Hay Papers.

[114] Ibid., 62–63.

[115] Linn, *Guardians of Empire*, 8–9.

[116] Ibid., 80.

[117] Braisted, *Navy in the Pacific, 1897–1909*, 63.

Pacific,"[118] and "the United States possessed no naval dry dock for its battleships on the Pacific

Coast save for the one dock at the small navy yard at Bremerton, Washington."[119] Even prior to

1903, the Navy's General Board considered Subic Bay in the Philippines as a possibility for a

base,[120] but in a period of limited resources, hard choices had to be made. A resolution by the

Army and Navy's Joint Board (subsequently approved by President Taft) included retaining "only

a small station at Olongapo" on Luzon for ship repair and "establishment of a reserve coal pile

and a naval magazine under the big guns at Corregidor." [121] This board's resolutions affected

Army basing as well. In 1909, it "concluded that no major war base should be built farther west

than Pearl Harbor."[122]

For naval leaders, Guam was another natural possibility—situated in a line drawn

between Hawaii and the Philippines through the central Pacific. According to Braisted, its

significance was noted by such leaders as Admirals Mahan and Winterhalter.[123] Braisted also

asserts that, "Neither the Philippines nor Guam could be considered independently of the

other."[124] The Navy began looking at it in 1909 as a potential "coaling station and cable

landing."[125]

Of course, the Department of the Navy was not the only player in these basing

discussions. The War Department had a say as well, and joint basing decisions could be

controversial. For example, there was some dispute between the services regarding the best

---

[118] Braisted, *Navy in the Pacific, 1897–1909*, 201.

[119] Ibid., 194.

[120] Braisted, *Navy in the Pacific, 1909–1922*, 5.

[121] Ibid., 64.

[122] Ibid.

[123] Ibid., 73, 257.

[124] Ibid., 246.

[125] Ibid., 72.

location on the Philippines to build a major port—notably between Subic Bay and Manila Bay.[126] A Joint Board settled on Manila Bay in 1908, but the importance of these decisions drew a number of players into the process—up to and including President Taft.[127] Braisted highlights the joint problems that can arise in this type of situation: "The disputes between the Army and the Navy over the Philippine base exemplify the lengths to which two armed services, or two bureaucracies, within a single government will go to defeat each other's objectives."[128] This illustrates some of the challenges involved in determining the proper location and disposition of facilities in the Asia–Pacific region in this period.

Planners could not afford to ignore or marginalize the importance of bases and facilities. Braisted underscores this importance by asserting that this was the "basic problem that influenced American naval policy in the Pacific throughout the period of this study [1909–1922]: the development of bases and other forms of support that would enable the United States to dispatch and maintain a fleet in the western Pacific sufficiently powerful to win naval dominance in those waters from Japan."[129]

Clearly "facilities" was a critical variable that affected operational risk. The overall U.S. capability gap and level of exposure was not tested until the 1940s. But, it seems clear that facilities challenges—given the fiscal constraints and interservice disagreements—raised operational risk during the period of this case study.

---

[126] Braisted, *Navy in the Pacific, 1909–1922*, 61–62.

[127] Ibid., 61–62, 69.

[128] Ibid., 71.

[129] Ibid., 35. Although this passage appears at the end of a chapter titled "The Taft Years, 1909–1913," Braisted is apparently referring to the period comprising the years in the title of his book.

Analysis

This case study analyzed the increases in responsibility of the United States in the Asia–Pacific region following the addition of the Philippines as a U.S. territory in 1898. Events in later years—namely, U.S. losses to Japan in the Asia–Pacific region in the 1940s—suggest that the increase in responsibilities generated challenges that were not sufficiently mitigated within the variables discussed, leading to an overall increase in operational risk. There are a number of possible reasons for this.

First, even though the War Department and the Department of the Navy were the only two major military players, inter-service disagreements created difficulties in some of the DOTTF decisions, notably facilities. The fact that some decisions required horizontal consensus, and multiple vertical levels of approval up to and including the president, illustrates the challenges that complicated decision making. With the emergence of the Marine Corps as a distinct service (albeit with strong ties to the Department of the Navy) as well as an Air Force, the possibilities of similar inter-service rivalry causing challenges in similar situations in future years is evident.

Next, the operational planners in this case study sometimes worked without clear strategic guidance and objectives. Besides prolonging certain decisions, this could have also caused planners to make less than optimal choices. This illustrates the importance of clear strategic and political objectives for operational planners.

Finally, the increased responsibilities combined with a potential threat in this geographic region caused planners to investigate DOTTF and other solutions to mitigate operational risk. The environment they planned for—a region far from the American coast dominated by oceans, seas, and littoral regions—provided specific challenges for U.S. military leaders and planners. The most important DOTTF variables addressed in this case were organization and facilities.

"East of Suez" Case Study

The Indian Ocean region[130] is far from the continental United States; however, this factor did not diminish its importance for the United States as a global superpower in the wake of World War II. And the expeditionary wars that the United States has fought since then further illustrate its importance. Donald L. Berlin predicted in 2002 that, "Based on recent developments, it is likely that the Indian Ocean region will surpass [the Atlantic and Pacific] zones in importance in the 21st century."[131]

This case study analyzes the increase in U.S. military responsibilities in the Indian Ocean region after the British pulled out of the "East of Suez" area. It occurs primarily during the Cold War, starting at the end of WWII and ending with the fall of the Soviet Union in 1991. Although there have been changes to U.S. policy and facilities in the region after 1991,[132] the major perceived threat to U.S. interests in the Indian Ocean, the Soviet Union, expired with the end of

---

[130] This paper considers the Indian Ocean region as the ocean itself, adjacent seas, littoral countries, and the straits that access it. Rasul Rais provides the following useful description: "The Indian Ocean covers about 20 per cent of the total sea waters. Unlike the Atlantic and the Pacific, the Indian Ocean does not extend into the Northern hemisphere much farther than the Tropic of Cancer, The boundaries of the Indian Ocean are defined as follows: the border with the Atlantic is generally agreed to be at Cape Agulhas, on the southern tip of Africa, and it runs south along the 20 E meridian to the coast of Antarctica. The south-east boundary with the Pacific Ocean is usually drawn from the South East Cape, on the island of Tasmania, south along the 147 E meridian to Antarctica. The north-eastern border is the most difficult to define. The majority of researchers consider it to run across the Torres Strait between Australia and the island of New Guinea and then from the island of Adi, off the coast of Western New Guinea, along the southern shores of the Lesser Sunda islands and Java, then across the Sunda Strait to the shores of Sumatra." Rais, Rasul B., *The Indian Ocean and the Superpowers* (New Jersey: Barnes & Noble Press, 1987), 33. Yet, there are other countries and areas that affect the Indian Ocean and might be considered part of the region. Robert Kaplan states that, "The greater Indian Ocean region encompasses the entire arc of Islam, from the Sahara Desert to the Indonesian archipelago." Kaplan, Robert D., "Center Stage for the Twenty-First Century: Power Plays in the Indian Ocean," *Foreign Affairs* 88:2 (2009), Academic OneFile. http://go.galegroup.com.lumen.cgsccarl.com/ps/i.do?&id=GALE%7CA194963208&v=2.1&u=97mwrlib&it=r&p=AONE&sw=w (accessed 30 October 2011), No page.

[131] Donald L. Berlin, "Neglected No Longer: Strategic Rivalry in the Indian Ocean," *Harvard International Review* (Summer 2002), 31.

[132] See, for example, Ibid., 28. Berlin states that, "The United States began to build its existing Indian Ocean strategic infrastructure in the years following the 1991 Persian Gulf War, and has particularly expanded efforts since 1995 when the administration of President Bill Clinton shifted toward a more interventionist international policy."

the Cold War. Sandy Gordon states that actions up to the year 1988 "had created a new *détente* in superpower relations,"[133] and Berlin relates that certain United Nations committee members argued in 1989 that "superpower rivalry in the Indian Ocean had diminished with the end of the Cold War."[134]

The beginnings of U.S. involvement in the region

U.S. activities in the Indian Ocean region predate World War II. American presence in the region dates back to the "late eighteenth century," and U.S. involvement there increased during World War II.[135] But, according to Monoranjan Bezboruah, "as the war ended, the United States retreated into the Atlantic and the Pacific and left the Indian Ocean to the British"[136]

The United States did not lose interest in the region, however. Bezboruah states that, "The overwhelming concern of the United States, as the principal actor in the post-World War II international scene, was to contain the Communist expansion in Europe,"[137] and "the need to check Communist expansion … made the continued British presence in Singapore and Malaya mandatory."[138] Thus, while the British were doing their part to contain Communism in the Indian Ocean, the United States could focus similar efforts elsewhere. But this situation was not to last.

_____

[133] Sandy Gordon et al., *Security and Security Building in the Indian Ocean Region* (Canberra, Australia: Strategic and Defence Studies Centre, 1996), 37–38.

[134] Berlin, "Neglected No Longer," 26. Berlin is referring to "key Western members" who withdrew from the UN Ad Hoc Committee on the Indian Ocean, because the new dynamics of the "superpower rivalry in the Indian Ocean" rendered "a Zone of Peace purposeless."

[135] Bezboruah, *U.S. Strategy*, 33. In a note, Bezboruah points to the following source: U.S., Congress, House, Subcommittee on the Near East and South Asia, Committee on Foreign Affairs, *Proposed Expansion of U.S. Military Facilities in the Indian Ocean*, testimony of Seymour Weiss, 93d Congress, 2d Session, 1974, 22.

[136] Bezboruah, *U.S. Strategy*, 33.

[137] Ibid., 34.

[138] Ibid., 15. In a note, Bezboruah points to the following source: Robert Scott, *Major Theatre of Conflict: British Policy in East Asia* (London: Alliance Trade Study, 1968), 2.

British withdrawal and increase of U.S. responsibility

The 1956 Suez Crisis changed Britain's view on foreign policy. According to Bezboruah, it "was the watershed in British strategy."[139] It also affected the United States, as Bezboruah observed that it was likely the event "that finally persuaded Washington to look at the Indian Ocean region anew."[140] In the early 1960s, the United States began looking for potential bases in the Indian Ocean,[141] and "by 1964, the Indian Ocean decisively entered into America's calculations."[142] Yet, with the British presence the United States did not have a pressing need to commit significant resources in the region.

In the 1960s, the United Kingdom began sending signals that it was overextended. According to Rasul B. Rais, "As a result of economic pressures, Britain reviewed her security policy east of Suez, thus altering significantly a British-centred Western defence posture in this region."[143] In 1968, the United Kingdom "announced the decision to withdraw from east of Suez, paving the way for the so-called power vacuum in the region."[144] It would soon no longer be appropriate to call the Indian Ocean a "British lake."[145] The period of British primacy in the Indian Ocean was coming to an end.

---

[139] Bezboruah, *U.S. Strategy*, 16. In a note, Bezboruah points to the following sources: Richard N. Rosecrance, *Defense of the Realm: British Strategy in the Nuclear Epoch* (New York: Columbia University Press, 1968), 233; DewWitt C. Armstrong, "The British Re-Value Their Strategic Bases," *Journal of the Royal United Services Institution* (November 1969), 423.

[140] Ibid., 35.

[141] Ibid., 57; David Vine, *Island of Shame: The Secret History of the U.S. Military Base on Diego Garcia* (Princeton: Princeton University Press, 2009), 61.

[142] Bezboruah, *U.S. Strategy*, 60.

[143] Rais, *Indian Ocean and the Superpowers,* 41.

[144] Bezboruah, *U.S. Strategy*, xv.

[145] Dale R. Tahtinen and John Lenczowski, introduction to *Arms in the Indian Ocean: Interests and Challenges* (Washington D.C.: American Enterprise Institute for Public Policy Research, 1977). No page. The term "British lake" is seen in other works as well. See, for example, Bezboruah, *U.S. Strategy*, xvi.

This translated to an increase in responsibilities for the United States. Unfortunately, with the ongoing conflict in Vietnam, as well as domestic pressures, Britain's decision added an additional burden to the United States, and policymakers in Washington, among others, were outwardly unhappy with it.[146] 1968 heralded another significant event as well: it was the year that the Soviet Navy began a "regular presence" in the Indian Ocean.[147] Bezboruah states that this move "caught the United States unaware," and "was seen as part of a calculated Russian move to fill the vacuum created by the withdrawal."[148] This added further complexity to the situation. Rais tells us that, "In view of the British withdrawal, US policy-makers began to give serious thought to an American Indian Ocean policy that would demonstrate the vitality of the Western interest in the region."[149]

Basing solutions

In order for the United States to become a player in the Indian Ocean, it had to address the challenge of distance: the center of the Indian Ocean "is nearly exactly on the other side of the world."[150] To address this issue, the United States pursued a "strategic island concept," which relied on a "strong naval presence secured by firm control of the ingresses and egresses of the vital sea-lanes."[151] According to Bezboruah, this was "a preferable alternative to securing bases

---

[146] Bezboruah, *U.S. Strategy*, 27. For further discussion on this, see also, Kim C. Beazley, "The October War, the 1973–1974 Arab Oil Embargo, and U.S. Policy on the Indian Ocean," in *The Indian Ocean in Global Politics,* eds. Larry W. Bowman and Ian Clark (Boulder: Westview Press, 1981), 110–111.

[147] Ibid., xv.

[148] Ibid., 35.

[149] Rais, *Indian Ocean and the Superpowers*, 41.

[150] Howard Wriggins, "U.S. Interests in the Indian Ocean," in *The Indian Ocean: Its Political, Economic, and Military Importance,* eds. Alvin J. Cottrell and R.M. Burrell (New York: Praeger, 1972). 358.

[151] Bezboruah, *U.S. Strategy*, 227.

on the populated shores, which tended to generate 'problems.'"[152] To that end, U.S. planners

considered islands such as Diego Garcia and Aldabra.[153]

The Nixon Doctrine

President Richard Nixon's doctrine had significant effects in the Indian Ocean region. At

a press conference in Guam on 25 July 1969, Nixon made the following statement about U.S.

allies in the Asia–Pacific region:

> The political and economic plans that they are gradually developing are very hopeful.
> We will give assistance to those plans. We, of course, will keep the treaty
> commitments that we have. But as far as our role is concerned, we must avoid that
> kind of policy that will make countries in Asia so dependent upon us that we are
> dragged into conflicts such as the one that we have in Vietnam.[154]

These words, along with later remarks, were his first statements on what the press came

to call the "Nixon Doctrine."[155] According to Rais, one of its themes was to emphasize "a

balanced US role requiring increased sharing of the burden and responsibility by allies for their

own protection and a 'more equitable sharing of the material and personal costs of security.'"[156]

In short, the United States was looking for help from regional players to maintain stability in key

areas. This would have included the Indian Ocean region. Kim Beazley notes that an interest in

---

[152] Bezboruah, *U.S. Strategy*, 227.

[153] Rais, *Indian Ocean and the Superpowers,* 78. In a note, Rais points to the following work:
Exchange of Notes … Concerning the Availability of the British Indian Ocean Territory for Defence
Purposes. 3–11. Rais relates that, in "December 1966, Britain signed a defence deal with the United States
leasing the BIOT [British Indian Ocean Territory] for 50 years with the option of a further 20 years'
extension"; Vine, *Island of Shame*, 96.

[154] Richard Nixon, "Informal Remarks in Guam With Newsmen," 25 July 1969, *The American
Presidency Project* (by Gerhard Peters and John T. Woolley)
http://www.presidency.ucsb.edu/ws/?pid=2140 (accessed 16 February2012).

[155] Jeffrey Kimball, "The Nixon Doctrine: A Saga of Misunderstanding," *Presidential Studies
Quarterly* 36, no. 1 (March 2006), http://proquest.umi.com.lumen.cgsccarl.com/pqdlink?vinst
PROD&fmt=6&startpage=-1&vname=PQD&RQT=309&did=996135961&scaling=FULL&vtype=
PQD&rqt=309&cfc=1&TS=1329363739&clientId=5094 (accessed 15 February 2012), 60–64.

[156] As cited in Rais, *Indian Ocean and the Superpowers*, 47.

the protection of "Western interests" came with the policy, as well as a desire to lessen the chances that U.S. military forces would be needed in the region.[157] This desire to reduce the potential requirement for U.S. military involvement must be viewed in the context of the waning hours of the Vietnam conflict. Beazley notes this when she states that "the United States retained substantial forces in Southeast Asia for some time after the [Nixon] doctrine's enunciation."[158] Yet, the United States was not trying to relinquish its role as a global superpower. Bezboruah caveats that the doctrine "only emphasized other countries' contributions to the task of security and the maintenance of peace," and "did not try to reduce U. S. leadership."[159] The United States still recognized its increased responsibilities in the Indian Ocean region.

The post-Arab–Israeli War period

In October 1973, Egypt invaded the Sinai, initiating the Arab–Israeli war, the effects of which would ripple into the Indian Ocean as well. According to Dieter Braun, "The October 1973 war dramatically altered, for the first time, the strategic situation in the Indian Ocean, according it global significance."[160] It also shaped U.S. thinking about the region, as related by Bezboruah: "The Middle East War of 1973 is portrayed by the Defense Department as a watershed in U. S. strategic thinking about the Indian Ocean. The war transformed the traditional view of the Indian Ocean."[161]

---

[157] Beazley, "The October War," in Bowman and Clark, 109–110.

[158] Ibid., 109.

[159] Bezboruah, *U.S. Strategy*, 51.

[160] Dieter Braun, *The Indian Ocean: Region of Conflict or "Peace Zone"?* (New York: St. Martin's Press, 1983), 41.

[161] Bezboruah, *U.S. Strategy*, 68. In a note, Bezboruah points to the following source: U.S., Congress, Senate, Committee on Foreign Relations, *Briefings on Diego Garcia and Patrol Frigate*, 93d Congress, 2d Session, 1974, 2. See also, Gordon et al., *Security Building*, 30. Gordon et al. state that, "From the perspective of the United States, the 1973 war increased substantially the salience of the Indian Ocean in strategy."

The effects of the war on the U.S. policy in the Indian Ocean were evident. Diego Garcia expansion was prioritized,[162] and the United States sent "a carrier task force [to] the Indian Ocean in December 1973" to address the "lack of a coercive naval capability in the area."[163] The oil embargo that followed the conflict was also significant—bringing "the issue of oil supplies from the Persian Gulf into the forefront of Western priorities."[164]

Thus, we see in the aftermath of the Arab–Israeli War, an Indian Ocean that featured two superpowers—the United States and the Soviet Union—increasing their military activities and commitments. According to Berlin, in the 1970s (and 1980s), both powers "vied for political advantage, while their navies competed for refueling facilities and bases in places such as Socotra Island in the former South Yemen, Gan in the Maldives, and Port Victoria in the Seychelles."[165] It became a period where both of these players kept a wary eye on the Indian Ocean region, but in which it did not become a flashpoint—at least until 1979.

The Department of Defense viewed an Indian Ocean expansion period in the early 1970s to be "in tune with the Nixon Doctrine."[166] In retrospect, that move seems to have been appropriate, as the 1970s continued to exhibit a degree of turbulence. According to Braun, in the late 1970s, the U.S./U.S.S.R. rivalry operated at a "relatively low level" in the Indian Ocean, until "the Soviet and Cuban build-up of forces in the Horn of Africa."[167] And, along with losing Iran as

---

[162] Bezboruah, *U.S. Strategy*, 69. In a note, Bezboruah points to the *Military Procurement Supplemental FY 1974,* on S. 2999, 93d Congress, 2d Session, 1974, 54–55.

[163] Rais, *Indian Ocean and the Superpowers*, 49–50.

[164] Braun, *Indian Ocean*, 32.

[165] Berlin, *Neglected No Longer*, 26. A portion of the quoted text is italicized in the original— formatting in the article's lead paragraph.

[166] Bezboruah, *U.S. Strategy*, 52. In a note, Bezboruah points to the following source: William Beecher, "U.S. Move in Indian Ocean Is Linked to Commitments," *New York Times*, 8 January 1972, 10.

[167] Braun, *Indian Ocean*, 29.

"its most important regional ally"[168] from the Iranian Revolution, the U.S. suffered further

setbacks in the region in 1979. Larry W. Bowman and Jeffrey A. Lefebvre give these as, "conflict

between the two Yemens … petroleum shortages and the second major surge in prices … the

seizing of American hostages in Iran in November, and, finally … the Soviet invasion of

Afghanistan in December."[169]

American involvement in the region took a number of forms in 1979 and beyond. Braun

notes that conflict in southeast Asia drove the United States' "decision to step up a naval presence

in the Indian Ocean in early 1979."[170] But, instead of building new bases from the ground up,

U.S. leaders began looking for "access to already existing facilities"—such as Kenya, Oman, and

Somalia—to facilitate operations in the Indian Ocean.[171]

The events of 1973 and 1979 were like tectonic shifts in the region. The resulting

destabilization in its oil-producing areas was significant for U.S. policymakers, and a shift in U.S.

policy was not long in coming. William L. Dowdy and Russell B. Trood tell us that,

> In January 1980, in an important and much-quoted passage from his State of the
> Union address, President Carter replaced the moribund Nixon Doctrine with a doctrine
> of his own: 'Any attempt by any outside force to gain control of the Persian Gulf
> region will be regarded as an assault on the vital interests of the United States of
> America and such an assault will be repelled by any means necessary, including
> military force.'[172]

Carter followed his statements with action. Sandy Gordon reports that, after the Iranian

Revolution and Soviet invasion of Afghanistan, he "announced the creation of a Rapid

---

[168] Braun, *Indian Ocean*, 35.

[169] Larry W. Bowman and Jeffrey A. Lefebvre, "The Indian Ocean: U.S. Military and Strategic
Perspectives," in *The Indian Ocean: Perspectives on a Strategic Arena,* eds. William L. Dowdy and Russell
B. Trood (Durham: Duke University Press, 1985), 413–414. See also, Gordon et al., *Security Building*, 31.

[170] Braun, *Indian Ocean*, 29. In a note, Braun also points to M. Leifer, *Conflict and Regional
Order in Southeast Asia*, International Institute for Strategic Studies, London (Winter 1980), 17f.

[171] Bowman and Lefebvre, "The Indian Ocean," in Dowdy and Trood, 416.

[172] Ibid., 414.

Deployment Joint Task Force (the RDF) ... strengthened US naval forces in the Persian Gulf (MIDEASTFOR) from three to five warships and raised the frequency of naval deployments into the Indian Ocean."[173]

American interest in the region continued in the last decade of the Cold War. According to Bowman and Lefebvre, "Since the creation of the RDF, American forces have participated in three major exercises in Southwest Asia," and the "most ambitious U.S. exercise to date" was Operation Bright Star in 1982.[174] Braun reports that, "After the Reagan Administration came into office, the military build-up in the Gulf and Indian Ocean region received even greater priority."[175] New attention was given to bases in Diego Garcia, Egypt, Somalia, Kenya, and Oman, which was accompanied by a significant increase in spending for the region under President Carter.[176] In the 1980s, U.S. political and military leaders also looked at Ras Banas, Egypt, as a potential base for the RDF.[177]

Reasons for U.S. involvement

There were a number of reasons for U.S. involvement in the Indian Ocean region during the Cold War period. Perhaps the most important one—especially after the 1973 oil embargo—was the oil resources in the region. Larry W. Bowman provides support to this with the statement, "Oil issues provide[d] the most compelling concern."[178] Dowdy and Trood also point out that, in 1985, "American interests revolve around the need to ensure access to Persian Gulf oil for itself

---

[173] Gordon et al., *Security Building*, 31–32.

[174] Bowman and Lefebvre, "The Indian Ocean," in Dowdy and Trood, 431.

[175] Braun, *Indian Ocean*, 46.

[176] Ibid. In a note, Braun also points to the following source: Newsom, (noted as a "former US Under-Secretary of State" by Braun on page 45) "testifying before the Senate Sub-committee on the Middle East and South Asia," in *USWB*, 13.3.1981, 12.

[177] Bowman and Lefebvre, "The Indian Ocean," in Dowdy and Trood, 421.

[178] Larry W. Bowman, introduction to *Indian Ocean in Global Politics*, Bowman and Clark, 1.

and its allies."[179] Closely related to this was a general U.S. economic interest in the region.

Bezboruah stated that, "economic considerations transform[ed] the U. S. quest for a strategy in

the Indian Ocean from a purely military matter into a broad policy concern."[180] Beazley

downplays the role of superpower rivalry for U.S. policy in the region with the statement that,

"Clearly, the economic stability of the West and the unity of the Western alliance were important

to the central balance."[181]

Stability and security were additional concerns in the area,[182] which certainly had the

potential to affect economic interests. For example, oil cannot be exported, and commercial trade

cannot flourish without safe passage through sea lanes. Rais stated that, one of "the US security

interests in the Indian Ocean," was "the safeguarding of the Sea Lanes of Communications."[183] In

Mahanian fashion, Ashok Kapur states that, "it is necessary to possess a capacity for 'sea control'

or 'sea denial' in the entire ocean to satisfy that interest."[184] Dowdy and Trood identify some of

the most critical sea straits and chokepoints in the region as the Straits of Malacca, Bab el-

Mandeb, and Hormuz.[185]

---

[179] Dowdy and Trood, *Indian Ocean: Perspectives*, 397. The authors do not state the year, but the book was published in 1985. Dieter Braun also notes that the State Department listed "oil from the Persian Gulf" as one of the "priority interests of the United States" in 1971: Braun, *Indian Ocean*, 30. See also, Rais, *Indian Ocean and the Superpowers*, 4; Ashok Kapur, "Carter's Diplomacy and the Indian Ocean Region," in *Indian Ocean in Global Politics*, eds. Bowman and Clark (Boulder: Westview Press, 1981), 136; Beazley, "The October War," in Bowman and Clark, 126.

[180] Bezboruah, *U.S. Strategy*, 42.

[181] Beazley, "The October War," in Bowman and Clark, 112.

[182] Rais, *Indian Ocean and the Superpowers*, 57, 62.

[183] Ibid., 62. For the importance to the U.S. of free movement through the region's sea routes, see also, Braun, *Indian Ocean*, 31; Bezboruah, *U.S. Strategy*, 36; Dowdy and Trood, *Indian Ocean: Perspectives*, 397–398.

[184] Kapur, "Carter's Diplomacy," in Bowman and Clark, 134. Bezboruah related control of Indian Ocean region to Mahan's ideas: Bezboruah, *U.S. Strategy*, 38.

[185] Dowdy and Trood, *Indian Ocean: Perspectives*, 397–398.

Strategic Context

The strategic context under which operational planners worked offers some useful lessons. It illustrates the difficulties that ensue when vague and/or unclear strategic guidance is provided. In the Indian Ocean region, the increase in U.S. military responsibilities combined with the challenge of generally unclear strategic guidance could have contributed to an increase in operational risk.

There were significant ambiguities in U.S. Indian Ocean policy in the period prior to the Arab–Israeli War. Kim Beazley notes that, "From the time of the announcement in 1968 by the British government of its intention to withdraw from the Indian Ocean region, U.S. policy has been characterized by hesitant attempts to define, in an unfamiliar area, the nature and significance of U.S. interests and the appropriate means of defending them."[186] During a critical time when U.S. operational planners were considering basing options, the Nixon Doctrine (as previously noted) signaled a desire for the U.S. to avoid potential military engagement in the region. During this same time, U.S. civilian leaders apparently thought that "no naval expansion was necessary for the security interests of the United States in and around the ocean."[187] Rais points out the development of Diego Garcia in pursuit of U.S. strategic goals, but also states that, "On the whole … the American presence during this period (1968–73), remained far less than adequate deterrence, because US naval policy in the Indian Ocean was still in a formative phase."[188] The lack of imminent threats may have contributed to an apparent laxity in establishing

---

[186] Beazley, "The October War," in Bowman and Clark, 108.

[187] Bezboruah, *U.S. Strategy*, 93. In a note, Bezboruah points to various sources for "testimonies": U.S., Congress, House, Subcommittee on National Security Policy and Scientific Developments, Committee on Foreign Affairs, *The Indian Ocean: Political and Strategic Future*, 92d Congress, 1st Session, 1971; U.S. Congress, House, Subcommittee on the Near East and Sourth Asia; Committee on Foreign Affairs, *Proposed Expansion of U.S. Military Facilities in the Indian Ocean*, 93d Contgress, 2d Session, 1974, testimony of Admiral Gene LaRoque.

[188] Rais, *Indian Ocean and the Superpowers*, 48–49.

clear policy objectives. In May 1974, retired Rear Admiral Gene La-Rocque summarized past U.S. policy in the Indian Ocean as—for the most part—"sound and reasonable, one of restraint and constrained military presence," because the United States had "no vital interests at stake in the region and … US security interests there are comparatively limited."[189]

The Arab–Israeli War provided the emphasis for a clearer strategic framework—at least in the near term. Bezboruah related a Congressional view that "the United States believes that neither its interests nor those of its littoral friends and allies would be served by a supposed U.S. inability to operate effectively in the waters."[190] Bezboruah's statement in his 1977 book highlights a concern for greater clarity in political guidance: "While negotiations for an [arms control] agreement are under way, the United States can gain additional diplomatic and political leverage by unilaterally issuing an Indian Ocean military posture statement. In the absence of such efforts, the Indian Ocean will become the center of intensified great-power rivalries and the scene of ever-increasing deployments of military might, possibly leading to a calamitous military confrontation."[191]

The events of 1979 again brought U.S. foreign policy concerns in the region. And U.S. leaders did take action, as previously noted. However, the strategic guidance for U.S. forces was very broad: "In July 1980, the supreme allied commander, Atlantic, Admiral Harry D. Train, explicitly stated that the purpose of U.S. naval forces in the Indian Ocean was to maintain access to energy resources; to retain access to the region for political, economic, and military reasons;

---

[189] Gene LaRoque, "An Island Paradise for the Admirals," *Washington Monthly*, May 1974, 49, quoted in Alvin J. Cottrell and Walter F. Hahn, *Indian Ocean Naval Limitations: Regional Issues and Global Implications,* (New York: National Strategy Information Center, 1976), 16.

[190] Bezboruah, *U.S. Strategy*, 45. In a note, Bezboruah points to the following source: U.S., Congress, House, *Proposed Expansion of U.S. Military Facilities in the Indian Ocean,* testimony of Seymour Weiss, 93d Congress, 2d session, 1974, 27.

[191] Bezboruah, *U.S. Strategy*, 230.

and to support NATO by providing support for the allies' sources of energy."[192] Apparently, however, some observers thought our policy toward the region was sufficient. Rais said, "In my view, the United States has acquired sufficient power projection capabilities in the Indian Ocean, which far exceed any Soviet sea power at any given time."[193] This suggests that the United States had the *means* to pursue a clear foreign policy stance in the Indian Ocean, but not necessarily the desire to formulate the ends and ways to actively direct them in a focused manner.

There are indications that a hesitant policy framework continued into the 1980s as well. Ashok Kapur stated in 1981 that one possible assessment of the region is, "the U.S. noninvolvement posture at present is not a policy but the result of an inconclusive debate within the United States and weak U.S. leadership."[194] Rais adds that there are various reasons for "America's 'strategic neglect' of the Indian Ocean/Persian Gulf region."[195]

This is not to say that U.S. policy on the Indian Ocean region in this period was completely bankrupt. Certain policies set forth in the wake of the events of 1973 and 1979 provided operational planners with broad guidance and resources. But, operational planners appear not to have clearly understood what political objects they were pursuing.

---

[192] Bowman and Lefebvre, "The Indian Ocean," in Dowdy and Trood, 426. In a note, Bowman and Lefebvre also point to the following source: "Navies and Foreign Policy: SACLANT's Views," *Navy International* 85 (September 1980): 570.

[193] Rais, *Indian Ocean and the Superpowers*, 90.

[194] Kapur, "Carter's Diplomacy," in Bowman and Clark, 138. Kapur states, "The first assessment is that more U.S. talk of the Kissinger and Carter variety is a cover for a policy of noninvolvement in issues that do not affect U.S. interests. The United States mostly has important but not vital interests in the region. (The exception is oil.) The Carter policy is a continuation of the Nixon doctrine" (137).

[195] Rais, *Indian Ocean and the Superpowers*, 95. Rais also points to the following source: Thomas H. Moorer and Alvin J. Cottrell, "The Search for US Bases in the Indian Ocean: A Last Chance," *Strategic Review* 8 (Spring 1980): 3. The stated reasons are: "the non-existence of any meaningful relationship between visible US military power and regional political stability, the legitimacy of a Soviet naval buildup in view of its 'confrontation' with China, and the lack of a serious threat to Western economic interests."

Even some of the apparently laudatory policy evaluations of the period should give us pause. For example, Dowdy and Trood paint a positive picture of U.S. policies toward the region in the mid-1980s.

> Despite some inconsistencies, American policy makers convey both by their words and their deeds an overall perception of the interdependence of events in the Indian Ocean region. There is a recognizable framework for American policy in the area that, while arguably inappropriate to the political forces at work in the region, nevertheless suggests a coherent and comprehensive approach to the protection of American interests. Finally, it is noteworthy that the Soviet Union appears to recognize a certain coherence in American policy. In April 1979, *Pravda* referred to 'the defense line being created by the Pentagon along the Egypt-Israeli, Persian Gulf, Diego Garcia, Australian perimeter.'[196]

But isn't it possible that the coherent policy the Soviets mentioned was directed toward the wrong political aim?[197] Dowdy and Trood interpreted the existence of a coherent American strategy, but at the stake of "political forces at work in the region." Yet, if that "coherent and comprehensive approach" was directed toward the wrong political and strategic objectives, then it could have been well-focused on the wrong problem.[198] This monograph does not suggest that U.S. strategic goals were backward in this period—only that evaluations about "coherent" operational plans merit closer consideration to see if they are actually aimed at achieving strategic and political objectives.

---

[196] Dowdy and Trood, *Indian Ocean: Perspectives*, 11–12.

[197] Although the *Pravda* article uses the word "policy," it appears to refer to "the defense line being created by the Pentagon," which indicates the employment of a military strategy comprising operational plans.

[198] Modern U.S. Army doctrine addresses this with operational design by advising commanders to "solve the right problem": Department of the Army, *FM 5-0*, 3-5.

Key variables analysis

Doctrine

U.S. leaders made policy changes toward the Indian Ocean region, but there were few substantive changes to the U.S. military strategy there. What we saw, on the average, was simply an expansion of our naval routines into the Indian Ocean region. For example, Ashok Kapur states that, after the 1962 Sino–Indian War, "the U.S. Pacific Fleet began to make periodic visits to Indian Ocean ports."[199] After the Arab–Israeli War, "The US navy received instructions to conduct regular patrols" in the Indian Ocean.[200] Bowman and Lefebvre clarify that, in the 1970s, "the navy began to rotate task forces into the Indian Ocean about three times a year."[201] History does not provide a clear answer on whether these changes mitigated the operational risk incurred when the United States assumed additional responsibilities in the Indian Ocean region.

For the United States Army, this case study is similar to the first in that it made no sweeping doctrinal changes—at least not in response to the situation in the Indian Ocean region.[202] Thus, this variable's effect on operational risk is undetermined.

---

[199] Kapur, "Carter's Diplomacy," in Bowman and Clark, 135.

[200] Braun, *Indian Ocean*, 41.

[201] Bowman and Lefebvre, "The Indian Ocean," in Dowdy and Trood, 425.

[202] Although U.S. Army doctrine changed multiple times during the Cold War, the changes apparently were not driven by circumstances in the Indian Ocean region. Rather, the impetus for change resulted from the necessity to account for nuclear weapons on the battlefield, the Korean War and Vietnam conflict, the potential for conflict between NATO and WARSAW pact countries in Europe, and the Arab–Israeli War, among others. Kretchik, *U.S. Army Doctrine*, 158–220; Saul Bronfeld, "Did TRADOC Outmanoeuvre the Manoeuvrists? A Comment," *War & Society* 27, no 2 (October 2008): 115, http://www.tase.co.il/NR/rdonlyres/29165C6B-875F-4B92-ACFA-4ACC3739CAD0/0/Did_TRADOC_ Outmanoeuvre_ the_Manoeuvrists_ s.pdf (accessed 15 February 2012). In a note, Bronfeld points to the following source: Donn A. Starry, "Letter to Dr. Richard M. Swain, June 7, 1995," Starry Papers, Historical Office, Headquarters, US Army TRADOC, Fort Monroe, VA. 8.

Organization

Like the Philippine case study, the Indian Ocean region illustrates the primacy of naval power in this type of situation. According to a statement from a U.S. Congressional meeting, "With their flexibility, mobility, and relative independence from their location in international waters, the naval units seem to be uniquely suitable for the viable presence that the United States desires to provide in the area."[203] Bezboruah also mentions Washington's "post-Vietnam disenchantment with land-based involvement in Asia," stating that Vietnam was a cause for the "reemphasis on the navy."[204]

In 1949, "the United States established a small Middle East naval force, MIDEASTFOR," in Bahrain.[205] Bowman and Lefebvre stated that this force and periodic U.S. naval rotations covered the Indian Ocean into the 1970s "but there was still no permanent presence of any consequence" until 1979.[206] As early as 1962, there was discussion in the U.S. Navy about permanently establishing a U.S. Eighth Fleet in the Indian Ocean.[207] However, in 1983, the commander of the U.S. Pacific forces (CINCPAC) still covered both the Indian and the Pacific Oceans.[208]

The 1970s saw changes to U.S. posture in the region. Secretary of Defense Schlesinger stated in December 1973 that "US Navy vessels would visit the Indian Ocean regularly and that

---

[203] Bezboruah, *U.S. Strategy*, 52. In a note, Bezboruah points to the following source: U.S., Congress, Senate, Committee on Appropriations, *Department of Defense Appropriations FY 1972*, 92d Congress, 1st Session, 1972, Pt. 3, Navy, 30. In the note, Bezboruah states that, "In Admiral Zumwalt's words, the Nixon doctrine implies 'greater reliance on our mobile, controllable, and politically independent sea-based forces'" (55).

[204] Ibid., 50.

[205] Vine, *Island of Shame*, 56. See also, Dowdy and Trood, *Indian Ocean: Perspectives*, 451.

[206] Bowman and Lefebvre, "The Indian Ocean," in Dowdy and Trood, 425.

[207] Bezboruah, *U.S. Strategy*, 59. In a note, Bezboruah points to the following source: "Sino-Indian Conflict Draws Navy Eye," *Christian Science Monitor*, 22 December 1962, 5.

[208] Gordon et al., *Security Building*, 32.

the naval presence would be more frequent there than in the past."[209] In 1977, the U.S. military presence typically comprised "a task force headed by a guided-missile cruiser, escorted by destroyers and often by attack submarines."[210] When this was absent and a carrier task force was not present, the Indian Ocean region fell under the "American Middle East Force" in Bahrain.[211] This changed again in 1979 when "a clear decision had been made that the United States would henceforth sustain a 'permanent naval presence' in the Indian Ocean."[212] Bowman and Lefebvre relate how this took shape: "Throughout 1980 and well into 1981 there were always two carrier battle groups on station near the Persian Gulf; generally this meant approximately twenty-four men-of-war and supply ships were always in the region with additional supply ships anchored at Diego Garcia."[213] They add that, considering the combined assets of the Navy, Marines, and Air Force, "a considerable arsenal had been massed in the region."[214] And the presence of U.S. naval power did not soon abate. According to Bowman and Lefebvre, "one or two carrier battle groups remain[ed] permanently deployed in the Indian Ocean."[215] But there was a cost to pay for this presence. The Chief of Naval Operations, Admiral Thomas Hayward "stated that 'the U.S. Navy

---

[209] Rais, *Indian Ocean and the Superpowers*, 50. In a note, Rais points to the following source: *New York Times*, 2 December 1973.

[210] Tahtinen and Lenczowski, *Arms in the Indian Ocean*, 20.

[211] Ibid.

[212] Bowman and Lefebvre, "The Indian Ocean," in Dowdy and Trood, 426. In a note, Bowman and Lefebvre point to the following source: Richard Burt, "President, Under the Pressure of Crisis, Looking to New Foreign Policy Goals," *New York Times*, 9 January 1980,

[213] Bowman and Lefebvre, "The Indian Ocean," in Dowdy and Trood, 425. In a note, Bowman and Lefebvre point to the following sources: Richard Halloran, "U.S. Studying $1 Billion Expansion of Indian Ocean Base" *New York Times,* 6 April 1980; Jay Ross, "U.S. Navy Flotilla Adapting to New Mission in Indian Ocean," *Washington Post*, 3 February 1981; Michael T. Kaufman, "U.S. Naval Buildup is Challenging Soviet Advances in Asia and Africa," *New York Times*, 19 April 1981.

[214] Bowman and Lefebvre, "The Indian Ocean," in Dowdy and Trood, 425.

[215] Ibid.

is a one-and-a-half ocean navy with a three-ocean commitment,' "[216] illustrating that, even during the Cold War, military operational planners faced a limited resource pool.

Unlike the Philippines case study, air power became a factor in this geo-environmental change. Braun asserts that the Nixon Doctrine accentuated the importance of both the U.S. Navy and Air Force with its "concept of greater aloofness from regional conflicts."[217] Bowman and Lefebvre point to the U.S. ability "to airlift Marines or other manpower assigned to the RDF to [a] crisis area" in the region in the 1980s.[218] Finally, the Air Force began competing with the navy for facilities in the Indian Ocean region; the Navy wanted Diego Garcia, a base on an atoll near the center of the Indian Ocean, while the Air Force wanted Aldabra—on an atoll about 600 kilometers from the coast of Tanzania.[219] Apparently, with the advent of the air domain, the U.S. Navy now faces potential competition, of a sort, from other armed services in distant, geo-environmental changes.

The 1980s saw additional developments in organization. The RDF was finally realized at the beginning of 1983 when it "officially became a full-scale military command" under the U.S. Central Command.[220] Although not specifically allocated to the Indian Ocean, its focus in the Middle East[221] affected the Indian Ocean region—notably by influencing the Persian Gulf and its oil fields that fed the sea routes entering the Indian Ocean. In the 1980s, the United States also developed maritime prepositioning stocks of supplies sufficient for a marine amphibious brigade,

---

[216] As cited in Bowman and Lefebvre, "The Indian Ocean," in Dowdy and Trood, 426. Bowman and Lefebvre also point to the following source: Drew Middleton, "Navy's Plight: Too Many Seas to Cover," *New York Times*, 1 February 1981.

[217] Braun, *Indian Ocean,* 28. See also, Rais, *Indian Ocean and the Superpowers*, 47.

[218] Bowman and Lefebvre, "Indian Ocean" in Dowdy and Trood, 424.

[219] Bezboruah, *U.S. Strategy*, 60–61.

[220] Bowman and Lefebvre, "The Indian Ocean," in Dowdy and Trood, 429; Rais, *Indian Ocean and the Superpowers*, 53.

[221] Rais, *Indian Ocean and the Superpowers*, 6.

and began developing of Diego Garcia into a "permanent support base" from its previous function as a communications facility.[222] Given the relatively robust levels of military power available as a whole, as well as the relatively low levels of fiscal and political constraints on projecting power abroad during the Cold War, it appears that the U.S. military was able to reduce capability gaps and operational risk through its organizational structure.

Threat environment

As noted, the primary threat for the United States in the Indian Ocean region during the Cold War was the Soviet Union. The Soviet threat to U.S. interests in the region varied over time, however. According to Ashok Kapur, "In Middle East and South Asia military crises (1967, 1971, and 1973, for example) the deployment of U.S. naval forces was explained as a response to the Soviet threat and as U.S. support for its allies."[223] And, as previously discussed, "Britain's announcement of the end of her 'peace-keeping' role in the region" happened simultaneously with the Soviet naval entry into the Indian Ocean in 1968.[224] This must have been a matter of some concern to U.S. policy-makers and operational planners.[225]

Yet, some observers assert that the U.S. reaction to Soviet interests in the region has been overstated. Beazley states that, "The argument about the need to deny the Soviet Union any political advantage that might accrue from a monopoly of the naval presence in the area was not insignificant. It was, however, secondary to a concern that it is necessary to be able to influence

---

[222] Rais, *Indian Ocean and the Superpowers*, 53–54.

[223] Kapur, "Carter's Diplomacy," in Bowman and Clark, 136.

[224] Rais, *Indian Ocean and the Superpowers*, 42.

[225] "For example, "Ronald Spiers, then director of the State Department's Bureau of Political-Military Affairs, warned a congressional committee against 'the growing Soviet naval capability in reference to the so-called "choke points" which control ingress and egress to and from the Indian Ocean.'" As cited in Beazley, "The October War," in Bowman and Clark, 111.

the West's principal oil suppliers."[226] Beazley relates the assertion by Ronald Spiers, "then director of the State Department's Bureau of Political Military Affairs," that "Soviet action was highly unlikely."[227] This is echoed by Rais as well.[228]

Even in the 1980s, the Soviet Union was the only other player with military capabilities sufficient to challenge the United States in the region. According to Dowdy and Trood, neither Japan nor China "has yet displayed an interest in or a capability for projecting power into the Indian Ocean."[229] In a more abstract sense, U.S. leaders may have seen the threat to U.S. interests in the Indian Ocean area as Communism. At the least, the Indian Ocean was an arena in which the spread of Communism could be affected one way or the other. Yet, in the end, the Soviet threat was sufficient to raise the overall level of operational risk in the Indian Ocean, albeit perhaps not to the degree that Japan did in the Asia–Pacific region a half-century before.

Facilities

Bases and facilities are necessary for the United States to sustain operations on the other side of the globe. Even after WWII, U.S. leaders had kept the Indian Ocean region in mind. Bezboruah states that the United States kept Kagnew Base in Asmara, Ethiopia and the base in Bahrain.[230] However, the United States adopted an "island strategy," which was designed to "avoid the political sensitivities of land bases."[231] The base at Diego Garcia was to become the keystone of this system.

---

[226] Beazley, "The October War," in Bowman and Clark, 108.

[227] Ibid., 111.

[228] Rais, *Indian Ocean and the Superpowers*, 3–4.

[229] Dowdy and Trood, *Indian Ocean: Perspectives*, 399.

[230] Bezboruah, *U.S. Strategy*, 34.

[231] Rais, *Indian Ocean and the Superpowers*, 77.

The centrally-located base at Diego Garcia[232] aided the United States military in various ways. Although initially set up as a communications center,[233] it eventually expanded to provide a wide range of support services for U.S. military forces—especially after the events in Iran and Afghanistan in 1979.[234] It added a useful link in the logistics chain that previously stopped at Subic Bay.[235] Bezboruah notes that next-closest support bases for submarines were at Subic Bay (4,000 miles away) and Guam (5,000 miles away).[236] It could also support a carrier task force.[237]

Although Diego Garcia was undeniably a critical portion of the U.S. Navy's Indian Ocean infrastructure, the base was usable by other U.S. services as well. For example, it could support a wide array of aircraft, up to and including the B-52.[238] In later years, it would contain pre-positioned stocks sufficient to "support an eighteen-hundred-man Marine amphibious unit that is now permanently stationed in the Indian Ocean," and ships with equipment and supplies enough to "keep a twelve-thousand-troop brigade operational in battle for a month."[239]

---

[232] Braun provides the following description of Diego Garcia: "This horseshoe-shaped atoll, approximately 23 km. long and 8 km. wide, lies in the centre of the strategically important northern half of the Indian Ocean. It is 1,800 km. from India, 3,300 km. from both the Bab-el-Mandeb and Malacca Straits and 4,200 km. from Bahrain in the Persian Gulf. It belongs to the Chagos group of islands which form part of the British Indian Ocean Territory established in 1966." Braun, *Indian Ocean*, 40.

[233] Bezboruah, *U.S. Strategy*, 67.

[234] Braun, *Indian Ocean,* 40.

[235] Bezboruah, *U.S. Strategy*, 81.

[236] Ibid.

[237] Ibid., 84.

[238] Ibid. In a note, Bezboruah points to the following source: United Nations, General Assembly, Ad Hoc Committee on the Indian Ocean, Declaration of the Indian Ocean as a Zone of Peace, *Report of the Secretary-General Pursuant to Paragraphs 6 and 7 of General Assembly Resolution 3080 (XXVIII) (A/AC. 159/1)*, 12. See also, Bowman and Lefebvre, "The Indian Ocean," in Dowdy and Trood, 424.

[239] Bowman and Lefebvre, "The Indian Ocean," in Dowdy and Trood, 423. In a note, Bowman and Lefebvre point to Robert S. Dudney, "A Year After—New U.S. Role in Mideast," *U.S. News & World Report*, 3 November 1980; Charles W. Corddry, "U.S. Deploys 7 Shiploads of Gear in Indian Ocean," *Sun* (Chicago), 6 March 1980; Clementson, "Diego Garcia," 36–38; Halloran, "Special U.S. Force for Mideast"; Robert A. Manning, "Gearing Up for the 'Quick Strike,'" *Boston Globe Magazine*, 21 November 1982.

In short, Diego Garcia was a critical link in the United States' Indian Ocean regional infrastructure. Alvin J. Cottrell and Walter F. Hahn stated that, "Diego Garcia has become the symbol of American presence and perseverance in the area."[240] In the 1980s, significant funds were allocated for the enlargement of Diego Garcia.[241]

Regardless of its import, there were other U.S. facilities in the Indian Ocean besides Diego Garcia. Although, in the late 1970s, the U.S. infrastructure in the region consisted of Israel and an incomplete Diego Garcia for the most part,[242] the U.S. steadily addressed this sparse framework. In the 1980s, the former Royal Air Force base at Masirah Island (off the coast of Oman), was added to the list of facilities available to U.S. forces.[243] Rais also points out plans for a "brigade staging facility at Thumrait" (in Oman) and states that, "Other facilities in Oman that are available to the US include Tuff on the Gulf of Oman, Seeb airport, Salalah (airfield and port), Khasab (airfield) and Port Qaboos."[244] Other links in the U.S. regional framework have included "communications facilities in Ethiopia, Iran, and Australia,"[245] and access to bases in Egypt (such as Ras Banas), Kenya and Somalia (such as Berbera).[246] Rais notes that access to existing bases is crucial to the RDF since otherwise it could not conduct and sustain itself in the Indian Ocean region in case of armed conflict.[247] In all, this network of bases was adequate to

---

[240] Cottrell and Hahn, *Indian Ocean Naval Limitations*, 25. For further statements on the importance of the base, see also, Bowman and Lefebvre, "The Indian Ocean," in Dowdy and Trood, 435.

[241] Braun, *Indian Ocean*, 43; Rais, *Indian Ocean and the Superpowers*, 85–86.

[242] Bowman and Lefebvre, "The Indian Ocean," in Dowdy and Trood, 415.

[243] Rais, *Indian Ocean and the Superpowers*, 87.

[244] Ibid.

[245] Kapur, "Carter's Diplomacy," in Bowman and Clark, 135.

[246] Rais, *Indian Ocean and the Superpowers*, 54, 75, 88–89; Bowman and Lefebvre, "The Indian Ocean," in Dowdy and Trood, 421.

[247] Rais, *Indian Ocean and the Superpowers*, 76.

sustain American expeditionary forces and contributed to mitigating the operational risk the U.S. incurred when assuming responsibilities in the Indian Ocean region.

Analysis

This case study examined the history of the Indian Ocean region in the years 1945–1991, and looked at U.S. activities within a DOTTF framework. A number of themes and ideas are worth highlighting. First, technology was not a significant factor in addressing operational risk. The United States did not appear to pursue technology solutions specifically to address a geo-environmental change in the Indian Ocean region. This may have been because technology was not one of the drivers for the change—the increase in responsibilities in a new geographic region was. Second, the importance of the Indian Ocean to U.S. leaders in the period is obvious; but, it appears that strategic guidance was lacking. In this case, it seems that the United States had the means to engage firmly in the region—as one of the two global superpowers—but not necessarily the will that translated to clear ends and ways.

It is difficult to gauge the effectiveness of the U.S. military's operational planners in pursuing U.S. political and strategic objectives, such as they were. There was arguably no existential threat to the United States in the region, and there was no actual military conflict or confrontation as there was in the Asia–Pacific region when Japan attacked U.S. interests there at the outset of WWII. For various reasons, the Indian Ocean did not become a region of conflict for the two superpowers.

In any event, U.S. operational planners made some reasonable choices with the broad guidance they were given. Choosing an island strategy for basing avoided some of the potential regional conflicts that partly defined the littoral regions in this period. And the central location of Diego Garcia was beneficial for a number of obvious reasons. This facilities decision, along with the access to other bases in the region, may have mitigated a good deal of the operational risk incurred by a U.S. decision to become more engaged in the Indian Ocean. This case study also illustrates the importance of facilities to enable U.S. military operations in the region.

Finally, U.S. policymakers tended to be reactive in the region. Relatively strong, albeit expansive, policies were promulgated only after significant regional events—notably Britain's announcement to retrench, the 1973 Arab–Israeli War, and the events in Iran and Afghanistan in 1979. Broad policy guidance required operational planners to pursue plans that would allow the greatest flexibility in response to a regional crisis. As U.S. military forces in the region were not severely taxed or tested within this period, it is difficult to say whether this approach would have been successful in all possible scenarios.

Summary of the variables' effects on operational risk

In the first two case studies, the DOTTF variables affected operational risk to different degrees. The doctrine variable's effect on operational risk was negligible because no related sweeping doctrinal changes were made in either case. The organization variable contributed to an increase in operational risk in the Asia–Pacific case study, but did not in the Indian Ocean case. This is likely due to two causes, (1) the strain caused in the first case of adapting to a wholly new expeditionary concept, and (2) the relatively greater political and fiscal ability of the military to project force during the Cold War. In the second case, the United States was already a global power and had capabilities to project force into the Indian Ocean region without major changes.

The United States did not make major technological changes specifically to address the geo-environmental changes discussed in the Indian Ocean case study, and the notable technological change in the Asia–Pacific region case study apparently did not significantly reduce operational risk. As noted, this might be explained, at least in part, by the idea that technology has played a major part in driving RMAs in the past; but, in this case, the driver of these changes are increases in responsibilities in geographic regions. This is not to say that technology could not play a part in mitigating challenges encountered in geo-environmental changes; it simply was not a critical factor in addressing capability gaps and operational risk in these cases.

Both cases featured clear threats to U.S. interests, which raised the level of operational risk for the U.S. military. Concerning this variable, it is worth noting that the threats were conventional military threats. Military planners should not be surprised to see unconventional threats in future geo-environmental changes.

Finally, the facilities variable was critically important in both cases. This is understandable given the distances involved from the continental United States. However, the facilities employed by the United States military in the first case study did not appear to sufficiently address the challenges that Japan would present in the early portion of WWII. The absence of conflict in the Indian Ocean region suggests that the facilities were adequate to reduce the operational risk to U.S. forces.

Overall, the first two cases indicate that—in a situation with limited resources—a geo-environmental change increases operational risk. The cases suggest various factors that influence this risk. For example, the means available and the willingness of politicians to address resource shortfalls seem to be key considerations in the ability of the U.S. military to mitigate risk in these situations.

In the first case, the U.S. military did not, or was not able to adequately address the DOTTF variables, resulting in an increase in operational risk that was realized by combat losses in the 1940s. In the second case, it appears that the U.S. military was able to address the DOTTF variables sufficiently to reduce operational risk. Thus, the hypothesis that an increase in responsibility in a geographic region increases operational risk appears to be related to the degree to which the U.S. military can address the problem, given the means available, through the DOTTF and other variables. In the following case, this monograph analyzes the Arctic through this same framework to determine whether the U.S. military can mitigate operational risk within this framework.

The Arctic

The Cold War

Interest in the Arctic—for security purposes—dates back to the Second World War. Due to the difficulties of operating in the Arctic environment, it wasn't until that time that "the most advanced military powers were able to operate at the southern fringe of the area."[248] Later advances in technology during the Cold War allowed "weapons systems to operate in a sustained manner in the entire Arctic region."[249] Rob Huebert states that, "the Arctic was the critical strategic location for both fighting a nuclear war and avoiding it."[250] The attack warning needed by the U.S and Soviets to assist in deterrence, required "dependable observation systems as far north as possible."[251] But, after the Cold War ended, security-related interest in the Arctic seemed to wane. The Soviet Union, the United States, and other involved countries reduced their presence in the Arctic.[252]

In the 1990s, the Arctic stakeholders viewed the region differently. Some observers commented that it seemed like "a new and cooperative era was beginning."[253] Various Arctic

---

[248] Huebert, "Arctic Security Environment," 2. In a note, Huebert points to the following source: Mark Llewellyn Evans, *Great World War II Battles in the Arctic* (London: Praeger Publishers, 1999).

[249] Huebert, "Arctic Security Environment," 2.

[250] Ibid., 3.

[251] Ibid. Huebert also points to the following source: Harriet W. Critchley, "The Arctic," *International Journal* vol. XLII (Autumn 1987).

[252] Huebert, "Arctic Security Environment," 3–4. Huebert refers to the following sources: Oran Young, "Governing the Arctic: From Cold War Theatre to Mosaic of Cooperation," *Global Governance* vol. 11 (2005): 9–15; Rob Huebert "Canadian Arctic Security Issues: Transformation in the post-Cold War era," *International Journal* (Spring 1999).

[253] Huebert, "Arctic Security Environment," 4. Huebert states that, "The two leading scholars who have examined the developing cooperation in the region are Oran Young and Franklyn Griffiths" and lists the following sources: Oran Young, *Arctic Politics: Conflict and Cooperation in the Circumpolar North* (Hanover: University Press of New England, 1992); Oran Young, "Governing the Arctic: From Cold War Theatre to Mosaic of Cooperation," *Global Governance* vol. 11 (2005): 9–15, and Franklyn Griffiths ed. *Arctic Alternatives: Civility or Militarism in the Circumpolar North* (1992).

states, including Canada, Norway, and Denmark began cashing in their "peace dividend" following the Cold War.[254] The United States also reduced its Arctic infrastructure level in this period.[255] In 1996, the Arctic Council was created "to provide a means for promoting cooperation, coordination and interaction among the Arctic States."[256] By all accounts, the Arctic seemed to be becoming a region of peaceful cooperation.

This perception was not to last. Huebert states that, in 2005, the Arctic states seemed to have reevaluated their interests and their ability to act militarily in the region.[257] Besides most of these actors issuing "policy statements regarding Arctic security," Huebert states that, "Canada, Denmark, Norway, Russia and the United States have all either begun to rebuild their Arctic capabilities, or have indicated their plans to do so in the near future."[258] O'Rourke also notes the apparently shifting dynamics in the region, "Although there is significant international cooperation on Arctic issues, the Arctic is also increasingly being viewed by some observers as a potential emerging security issue."[259]

Interest in the region in the twenty-first century has not abated. Climate change is affecting the region,[260] and activity in the Arctic is increasing—"driven primarily by economic opportunity."[261] The Department of Defense further asserts that "human activity in the region will

---

[254] Huebert, "Arctic Security Environment," 3. Hubert points to the following work: Oran Young, "Governing the Arctic: From Cold War Theatre to Mosaic of Cooperation," Global Governance, Vol. 11 (2005): 9–15.

[255] Department of Defense, *Report to Congress*, 22.

[256] Arctic Council, *About the Arctic Council,* 7 April 2011, http://www.arctic-council.org/index.php/en/about (accessed 4 December 2011).

[257] Huebert, "Arctic Security Environment," 4.

[258] Ibid.

[259] O'Rourke, *Changes in the Arctic*, Summary (no page).

[260] Ibid., 8.

[261] Department of Defense, *Report to Congress*, 6.

increase over the coming decades."[262] The DoD assesses that there is "no current military threat in the region," but "competing economic and political interests resulting from changed conditions and increased human activity may result in disagreements between parties with competing interests."[263] The increased possibilities of the Arctic region, and the increase in human traffic that accompanies them, indicate a potential increase in responsibility for U.S. forces.

This potential increase in responsibility occurs in a period of limited and potentially declining resources. The Department of Defense's 2011 *Report to Congress on Arctic Operations and the Northwest Passage* notes "the many competing demands on DoD resources in the current fiscal environment."[264] Nevertheless, the Department of Defense believes that its current missions can be met with the capabilities on hand.[265]

The future for U.S. security interests in the Arctic is unclear, however. The DoD states that its current capabilities "will need to be re-evaluated as conditions change and gaps must be addressed in order to be prepared to operate in a more accessible Arctic."[266] Additionally, it is difficult to project what requirements the DoD will have in the Arctic decades from now. Huebert notes the "very early stages" of the regeneration of most of the Arctic states' operational capability.[267] However, it is difficult to determine to what end these buildups are aimed. Like the United States in the Indian Ocean case study, it could simply be preparation for crises, contingencies, and potential conflict. But, Hubert asserts that "it is hard to conceptualise what that conflict would look like. From a rational perspective, any conflict over resources would not

---

[262] Department of Defense, *Report to Congress*, 10. The original text was italicized.

[263] Ibid., 9.

[264] Ibid., 25.

[265] Ibid., 15.

[266] Ibid., 15–16.

[267] Huebert, "Arctic Security Environment," 2.

provide the 'winner' with meaningful gains."[268] In all, this illustrates a recurring challenge for

U.S. operational planners: how best to construct a campaign in a distant, geographic region with

limited infrastructure, nebulous threats, and an uncertain future? Any campaign must be

constructed with strategic and political goals in mind, so it is useful to examine these for the

United States in the Arctic region.

Strategic goals

The Department of Defense's 2011 *Report to Congress on Arctic Operations and the*

Northwest Passage appropriately lays out the political and strategic guiding documents for

military planners concerned with the Arctic. It states that "Strategic guidance on the Arctic is

articulated in National Security Presidential Directive (NSPD) 66 / Homeland Security

Presidential Directive (HSPD) 25, *Arctic Region Policy*. Additional guidance is found in the *2010*

National Security Strategy (NSS) and the *2010 Quadrennial Defense Review (QDR)*."[269]

According to the report, "The overarching strategic national security objective is a *stable and*

secure region where U.S. national interests are safeguarded and the U.S. homeland is

protected."[270] It also identifies a goal in NSPD-66 and HSPD-25 that "freedom of the seas" is a

"top national priority."[271] The United States' 2010 *National Security Strategy* has statements that

are pointedly relevant to the Arctic: "The United States is an Arctic Nation with broad and

fundamental interests in the Arctic region, where we seek to meet our national security needs,

---

[268] Huebert, "Arctic Security Environment," 22.

[269] Department of Defense, *Report to Congress*, 2. In a footnote, the report points out that, "The January 2009 National Security Presidential Directive (NSPD)-66, dual titled as Homeland Security Presidential Directive (HSPD)-25, or NSPD-66/HSPD-25, establishes the policy of the United States with respect to the Arctic region and outlines national security and homeland security interests in the region."

[270] Department of Defense, *Report to Congress,* 2. Italics in original .

[271] Ibid., 7.

63

protect the environment, responsibly manage resources, account for indigenous communities,

support scientific research, and strengthen international cooperation on a wide range of issues."[272]

The DoD's QDR identifies some blanket objectives that could also cover the Arctic, as

well as noting future possibilities for cooperation in the region.[273] Perhaps the most relevant

strategic guidance is the following in the DoD's *Report to Congress*: "*Prevent and deter* conflict

in the Arctic" and "*Prepare to respond* to a wide range of challenges and contingencies—

operating in conjunction with other states when possible, and independently if necessary."[274] Its

specific missions in the Arctic, as of 2011, are: "Maritime Domain Awareness," "Search and

Rescue," "Regional Security Cooperation," "Humanitarian Assistance / Disaster Response … &

Defense Support of Civil Authorities," "Maritime Security," "Power Projection," "Sea Control,"

"Strategic Deterrence," and "Air and Missile Defense."[275]

---

[272] United States, *National Security Strategy* (Washington D.C.: White House, 2010). http://www.whitehouse.gov/sites/default/files/rss_viewer/national_security_strategy.pdf (accessed 4 December 2011), 50.

[273] Department of Defense, *Report to Congress*, 8. The report stated the following: "Department of Defense strategic guidance was provided in the *2010 Quadrennial Defense Review (QDR),* which established four priority objectives for the Department: prevail in today's wars; prevent and deter conflict; prepare to defeat adversaries and succeed in a wide range of contingencies; and preserve and enhance the All-Volunteer Force. The QDR identified the opening of the Arctic waters for seasonal commerce in the decades ahead as 'a unique opportunity to work collaboratively in multilateral forums to promote a balanced approach to improving human and environmental security in the region.'"

[274] Department of Defense, *Report to Congress*, 8–9. Italics in original. In a footnote, the report also points to other sources: "The 2010 QDR Report states: 'America's Armed Forces will retain the ability to act unilaterally and decisively when appropriate, maintaining joint, all-domain military capabilities that can prevail across a wide range of contingencies.' This is consistent with NSPD-66/HSPD-25, which states: 'The United States has broad and fundamental national security interests in the Arctic region and is prepared to operate either independently or in conjunction with other states to safeguard these interests.' "

[275] Department of Defense, *Report to Congress*, 29–32. The report notes that analysis of Coast Guard missions is not included in the list; they will appear in the Coast Guard's "2011 High Latitude Study."

Key variables analysis

Doctrine

The United States military is no stranger to operating in cold weather environments, and the U.S. services conduct cold weather and Arctic training to validate current procedures. For example, "A periodic Ice Exercise (ICEX) is conducted by Commander, U.S. Submarine Forces, in order to validate submerged operations and tactics in the Arctic environment."[276] U.S. Army forces are also stationed in and train in Alaska.[277] Yet, save for a recently updated Army doctrinal publication, *Cold Region Operations* (2011),[278] no calls for a doctrinal overhaul are evident. Similar to the first two case studies, it is difficult to determine the doctrine variable's affect on operational risk in the Arctic. However, the distances involved, the scarcity of support infrastructure, and the unforgiving climate of the Arctic create specific challenges for military forces operating in the Arctic that could strain our current doctrine.

Organization

The organization of the U.S. armed forces may be one of the variables that contribute most to the increase in operational risk. A number of factors are involved. First, the Coast guard possesses the only U.S. government icebreaking capability.[279] This creates some challenges, such as how to plan for Search and Rescue (SAR) operations—one of the DoD's stated missions in the Arctic. Although SAR is "not a force sizing or shaping mission for DoD" and requirements and

---

[276] Department of Defense, *Report to Congress*, 17.

[277] Ibid.

[278] Department of the Army, *ATTP 3-97.11: Cold Region Operations* (Washington: Headquarters, Department of the Army, 28 January 2011).

[279] Department of Defense, *Report to Congress*, 27.

availability drive DoD's potential participation in Arctic SAR, the DoD's *Report to Congress* notes that, "The extreme distances, limited infrastructure, and paucity of assets will make a timely SAR response challenging in the best of conditions. As human activity increases in the region, this gap is expected to increase."[280] Second, although U.S. submarines have "been operating in the Arctic since the trans-Arctic voyage of USS NAUTILIS in 1958," our surface naval vessels "are not ice-strengthened" and face challenges in operating in the Arctic.[281] The Department of Defense noted that its "lack of surface capabilities able to operate in the marginal ice zone and pack ice will increasingly affect accomplishment of this mission area over the mid- to far-term."[282]

The lack of vessels capable of operating in the Arctic is concerning. According to the Department of Defense, "There are no U.S.-flagged heavy icebreakers in the U.S. commercial fleet. The U.S. Government inventory of polar icebreakers resides entirely within the U.S. Coast Guard."[283] And all of the Coast Guard's polar icebreakers are based in Seattle, Washington,[284] which means that they cannot influence U.S. interests in the eastern Arctic region without a long ocean voyage. According to a 2007 National Research Council report, the status of our current icebreaker fleet means that "U.S. [polar] icebreaking capability is now at risk of being unable to

---

[280] Department of Defense, *Report to Congress*, 14.

[281] Ibid., 17.

[282] Ibid., 15. The report notes that "the 'marginal ice zone' refers to the area between the pack ice and the open ocean that contains broken ice and is affected by wave action" (15). It also states that, "USTRANSCOM assesses that until navigational charts, aids to navigation, ice breaking support, and port infrastructure (including refueling capabilities) are more developed in the region and the United States procures strategic sealift vessels rated for operations in the Arctic, it is unlikely that DoD strategic sealift will be able to operate in the Arctic" (22).

[283] Ibid., 27.

[284] Martin Kaste, "In The Arctic Race, The U.S. Lags Behind," August 19, 2011, http://www.npr.org/2011/08/19/139681324/in-the-arctic-race-the-u-s-lags-behind (accessed 1 December 2011).

support national interests in the north and the south."[285] In an era of limited resources,[286] the Coast Guard faces potential challenges with its icebreaking capability.

There is another aspect of the U.S. military's organization that has the potential to affect operational risk. As of 6 April 2011, NORTHCOM now has responsibility for "the North Pole and its surroundings," although it will share responsibility in the region with EUCOM.[287] The DoD notes that this "makes coordination more challenging," but the alternative also has drawbacks.[288]

As stated, the DoD indicates that the problem is not currently pressing. However, the projected increase in activity in the Arctic in the future suggests that a capability gap will begin to emerge, leading to an increase in operational risk. How the gap will emerge, and how the U.S. military's operational planners account for it in an era of fixed and perhaps even declining resources is still unclear. What is clear is that the United States will be hard-pressed to reduce operational risk within the organization variable given current fiscal constraints.

Technology

It is difficult to imagine that, in the 21st Century, technology gaps could lead to an increase in operational risk in the Arctic operating environment. But, this could be a real concern for the U.S. military in the Arctic. It is true that, besides a few specific Arctic systems, there are vehicles and equipment in the U.S. inventory that can operate in the Arctic, including "P-3

---

[285] National Research Council, *Polar Icebreakers in a Changing World, An Assessment of U.S. Needs* (Washington, 2007), 2, quoted in O'Rourke, *Changes in the Arctic,* 31.

[286] Department of Defense, *Report to Congress,* 12. The original text is italicized.

[287] Jim Garamone, "Unified Command Plan Reflects Arctic's Importance," *Defense.gov,* 7 April 2011, http://www.defense.gov/news/newsarticle.aspx?id=63467 (accessed 3 December 2011).

[288] Department of Defense, *Report to Congress,* 3. The report states, "having too few [Combatant Commanders] would leave out key stakeholders, diminish long-standing relationships, and potentially alienate important partners."

Maritime Patrol Aircraft, F-22 Raptors, and Stryker vehicles, among others."[289] However, the DoD notes a potential need to continue developing "capabilities and capacity to defend U.S. air, land, and sea borders in the Arctic," and further states that, "The ability to locate, identify, and track surface vessels in the Arctic today is limited."[290] The DoD has identified three "capability gaps" that "have the potential to hamper Arctic operations": (1) "extremely limited" communications above 70°N latitude, (2) degraded GPS performance, and (3) limited "awareness across all domains in the Arctic."[291] This suggests that technological challenges, including the U.S.'s ability to apply technology to the challenges in the region, might contribute to an increase in operational risk in the region in the future.

Threat

Unlike the Asia–Pacific and the Indian Ocean region case studies, there is no single state actor with conventional military forces that presents a distinct threat to the United States in the Arctic. And the likelihood of "armed conflict" in the region has been assessed as "low" by the DoD.[292] But, state actors are not the only threat to consider in the Arctic. The DoD has identified "a range of other potential national security challenges, including smuggling, criminal trafficking, and terrorism."[293] This indicates that significant operational challenges could result simply from an increase in activity in the Arctic. The DoD describes this change as follows:

---

[289] Department of Defense, *Report to Congress*, 13. The DoD report notes the "few niche capabilities specifically tailored for Arctic Operations" as "the ski-equipped HC-130 Hercules aircraft and the '688i' LOS ANGELES-class submarines designed for under-ice operations with diving planes on the bow rather than on the sail, and reinforced sails."

[290] Ibid., 9, 14.

[291] Ibid., 16.

[292] Ibid., 13.

[293] Ibid., 7. In a note, the report states, "This report was informed by classified threat assessments by the National Intelligence Council, the Central Intelligence Agency, the Defense Intelligence Agency, and the Office of Naval Intelligence."

Economic viability of commercial ventures in the Arctic (e.g., oil and gas exploration, mineral extraction, tourism, and fishing) will be the dominant driver of the pace at which human activity increases in the region. Changes are expected to occur gradually and unevenly, driven by existing infrastructure, individual national policy decisions, and the self-interest of commercial entities, among other factors.[294]

The potential threats to U.S. national security in the Arctic are difficult to predict, both in nature and effect. Yet, it seems clear that the predicted increases in human activity in the Arctic may translate to a variety of threats that could lead to an increase in operational risk for U.S. forces.

Facilities

The western Arctic, (that is, the area centered on Alaska for the United States), contains the majority of U.S. facilities. Alaska is the United States' membership card as an Arctic State, and encompasses a number of military installations below the Arctic Circle, including Clear Air Force Station, Eareckson Air Station, Eielson Air Force Base, Fort Wainwright, Fort Greely, and Joint Base Elmendorf-Richardson.[295] Dutch Harbor, in the Aleutian Islands, is also close enough to influence the United States' western Arctic region.[296] Yet, the lack of a U.S. deep-water port in northern Alaska may be an area of concern. Senator Lisa Murkowski of Alaska believes that the United States needs "a deep-water port on Alaska's north shore."[297]

The U.S. military operates only one base north of the Arctic Circle—Thule Air Base in Greenland.[298] It boasts "the world's northernmost deep-water port, [and] a 10,000-foot runway."[299] Another facility available for Arctic aviation assets is Stratton Air National Guard

---

[294] Department of Defense, *Report to Congress*, 19.

[295] Ibid., 15, 18, 23.

[296] Ibid., 23, 24.

[297] Kaste, *Arctic Race*.

[298] Department of Defense, *Report to Congress*, 21. However, the diagram in the DoD's report shows U.S. Air Force radar sites above the Arctic Circle in Alaska.

[299] Ibid., 18.

Base in Scotia, New York.[300] Use of allied bases is also possible to address U.S. security interests

in the Arctic. For example, a former Air Force Base—Sondrestrom Air Base in Kangerlussuaq,

Greenland—"remains available for scheduled U.S. military flights and contingency

operations."[301] Thule AFB, along with support from Allied nations, is what the United States has

available to support military operations in the "eastern Arctic" area.[302]

Notwithstanding the current facilities available, "limited shore-based infrastructure" is

one of the challenges identified by the DoD in the region,[303] and "demand for supporting

infrastructure (e.g., ship repair and refueling facilities) will likely outpace availability."[304]

Various factors suggest challenges for operational planners in addressing facilities shortfalls in

the region. First, construction in the Arctic is difficult; it is a seasonal affair hampered by ice

movement that normally precludes "conventional pier construction," and is further complicated

by atypical hours of daylight and darkness.[305] Second, there are "long lead times for construction

of major infrastructure in the region."[306] Finally, the Department of Defense understands the

resource constrained environment it operates within: "The near-term fiscal and political

environment will make it difficult to support significant new U.S. Government investments."[307]

With these issues in mind, the Department of Defense cautiously determines that the "existing

DoD posture in the region is adequate to meet near- to mid-term U.S. defense needs," but "DoD

---

[300] Department of Defense, *Report to Congress*, 18.

[301] Ibid.

[302] Ibid., 23. Defined in the DoD report as "Baffin Bay plus the Greenland, Norwegian, and Barents Seas."

[303] Ibid., 3.

[304] Ibid., 12.

[305] Ibid., 24.

[306] Ibid., 3.

[307] Ibid., 12. Original italicized.

will periodically re-evaluate this assessment as the Combatant Commanders update their regional

plans on a regular basis."[308] As the ability of current U.S. facilities to sustain military operations

in the long-term is uncertain, the facilities variable may contribute to an increase in operational

risk as U.S. responsibilities in the region increase.

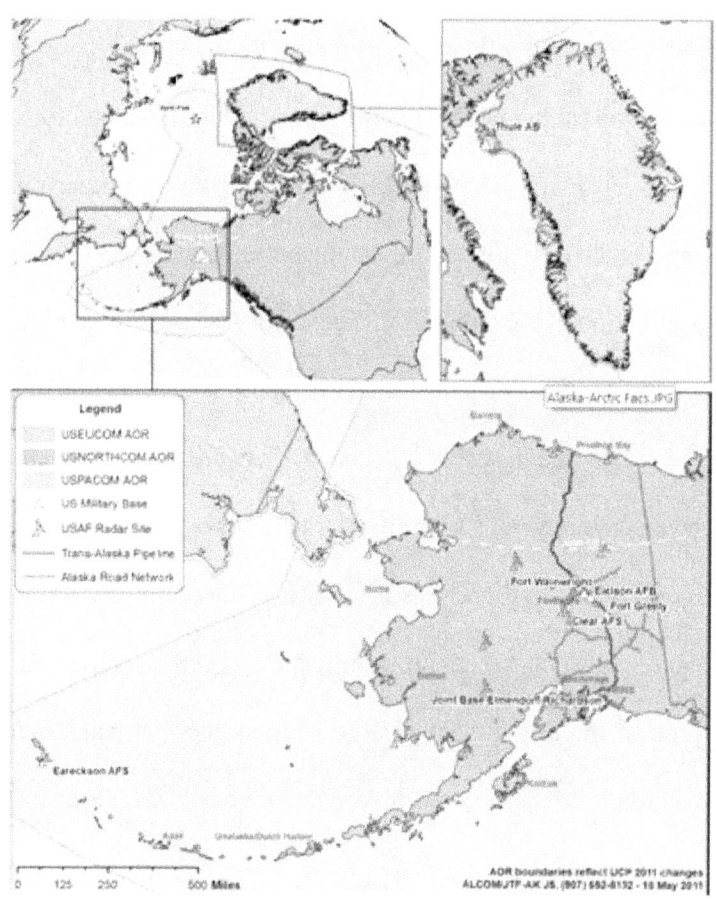

Figure 1. "Existing DoD Bases and Facilities in Alaska and the Arctic."[309]

---

[308] Department of Defense, *Report to Congress*, 3. The report "assesses major defense infrastructure, such as bases, airfields, and ports. Minor modifications to existing bases, such as the addition of a new hangar, will be made as part of the maintenance and modernization process."

[309] Ibid., 21.

Analysis

This case study examines the Arctic region's history from World War II to the current day. The analysis within the DOTTF framework reveals some useful areas for analyzing operational risk in the region. These areas are listed below.

The current military doctrinal definition of operational risk is the "probability and severity of loss linked to hazards."[310] In this light, current doctrine may be sufficient to support the current low tempo of U.S. military Arctic operations. The U.S. military's organization and technological state, although perhaps insufficient to deal with significant and sustained challenges in the Arctic, seems likewise to be sufficient to keep up with the current pace of Arctic operations. Given that the U.S. military has access to allied military bases to supplement its own, the facilities framework possessed by the United States military also appears to be adequate to support the DoD's current missions in the Arctic at a basic level. However, if the United States pursues conflicting Arctic claims with Allied states that offer basing rights to the United States, there is a potential for U.S. capability to project and sustain forces in the region to drop.

Overall, the reason that operational risk seems to be offset by the current capabilities of the U.S. military may be due, in part, because the threat to U.S. interests in the region is as yet ill-defined (between state and non-state actors), nebulous, and difficult to predict—both in nature and effect. However, as activity increases, capability gaps are likely to emerge, straining the U.S. government's (that is, the DoD and Coast Guard) capabilities in relation to their stated missions in the Arctic as structured within strategic and political objectives. This analysis suggests that an increase in U.S. military responsibility in the Arctic region may lead to an overall increase in operational risk.

---

[310] Department of Defense, *JP 1-02*, 297.

Analysis across the cases

This analysis examines the DOTTF variables across the case studies, and then discusses general trends that the case studies have illustrated. In both cases, lessons and information are drawn out that are relevant to operational planning for a geo-environmental change.

Doctrine, although an important factor in Revolutions in Military Affairs, played a relatively insignificant role in the geo-environmental changes analyzed. But it was certainly not nonexistent. In the Philippines case study the U.S. military added an expeditionary aspect to a predominantly continental defense force. Yet—perhaps given the scale and nature of the geo-environmental changes discussed—doctrinal changes seemed to affect operational risk relatively less than other variables.

Organizational challenges appear to have influenced operational risk in the first two case studies. In the Asia–Pacific region in the early 1900s, the U.S. military suffered from limited resources and the requirement to build a bridge, so to speak, to support operations in a new and distant theater of operations. The challenge of doing so while (1) addressing what was seen to be the primary concern of the United States—Europe—and (2) facing a limited resource pool, seems to have increased operational risk. Organizational challenges were seen again, albeit to a lesser degree, in the Indian Ocean region. Here, organizational solutions were likely hampered by a relative focus of resources on other areas such as the standoff with the Soviets in Europe and the struggle to contain Communism in Vietnam. Organizational challenges may be most evident in the Arctic however. Although there is no single, identifiable existential threat to U.S. interests in the Arctic, the ability of the United States to deal with a full spectrum of possible contingencies in the region in the future is concerning given the current organization of the United States armed forces—including the Coast Guard. In this light, organizational challenges should be a key planning consideration for operational planners in geo-environmental changes.

Although the Asia–Pacific case featured some relevant and notable technological changes, technology was apparently not a significant factor in decreasing operational risk in the analyzed geo-environmental changes. As noted, this might be because technology has historically been a *driver* in RMAs, whereas in geo-environmental change it seems be a post hoc effect in operational risk after the change has occurred. Additionally, that effect—at least in the cases analyzed here—has apparently been negligible in mitigating operational risk from a geo-environmental change. In the case of the Arctic, the relative lack of an ability to apply technological solutions might actually increase operational risk, although it is difficult to say to what degree since the same limiting factors that apply to U.S. military forces will likely apply to other actors in the region as well.

Although it may seem self-evident that threat would affect the level of operational risk in any environment, in this case, the concern is how threat might increase operational risk in geo-environmental changes beyond operational planner's ability to mitigate it. In the Philippines case study, the threat was apparently not mitigated sufficiently by operational plans, as indicated by events in the 1940s. Although there was no event that strenuously tested American power in the Indian Ocean during the Cold War, the threat did not appear to be more than operational planners could mitigate. The ability of American operational planners to address the threats in the Arctic is as yet unclear. Overall, in an Arctic geo-environmental change, and given limited resources, it appears that threat levels could increase operational risk beyond the ability of U.S. operational planners to address.

One of the clearer trends that can be elicited from this work is the importance of the facilities variable in a geo-environmental change. The varying ability of the United States to address this variable, combined with interservice rivalries, caused disparate outcomes in operational risk levels. In the Arctic region, an increase in responsibilities might well overstrain the United States' existing facilities ability to support full spectrum operations in the region—resulting in an increase in operational risk.

74

An additional consideration is that, given the significant costs of constructing new facilities in time, money, and political capital, in regions far from the U.S. continental shores, the United States may need to rely more on basing rights with allied nations in geo-environmental changes. Although the United States built new bases in support of the Asia–Pacific region in the early 20th century, the Indian Ocean case study illustrated a willingness of the United States to rely on allies for support in projecting military force. Given the difficulties in construction in the Arctic, as well as the limited resources available, operational military planners may need to increasingly investigate allied basing possibilities instead of pursuing purely U.S. bases and facilities. This may be a further indication that, in today's era of limited resources, the importance of alliances and partners as noted in the Secretary of Defense's January 2012 guidance to the United States military[311] may become increasingly relevant for the United States to project influence—assuming U.S. national ambitions do not change.

For U.S. planners seeking to further analyze these cases within doctrine, a number of the elements of operational design are relevant.[312] First, in a geo-environmental change, the lack of a clear *military end state* is difficult to overcome. This challenge was illustrated in the Asia–Pacific region for some time. It was also featured, to some degree, in the Indian Ocean region. For the Arctic region, a clear military end state will greatly assist planners in making crucial operational decisions to mitigate risk. Second, the importance of *lines of operation* to project force to distant geographic regions should be clear to U.S. planners. The types of geo-environmental changes discussed here emphasize the critical importance of lines of operation to supply joint forces for

---

[311] Department of Defense, *Sustaining U.S. Global Leadership: Priorities for 21ˢᵗ Century Defense* (Washington: Secretary of Defense, 5 January 2012), *www.defense.gov*, http://www.defense.gov/news/Defense_Strategic_Guidance.pdf (accessed 19 January 2012), 1–3, 5.

[312] U.S. joint doctrine gives the elements of operational art as "Termination," "Military end state," "Objective," "Effects," "Center of gravity," "Decisive point," "Lines of operation and lines of effort," "Direct and indirect approach," "Anticipation," "Operational reach," "Culmination," "Arranging operations," and "Forces and functions": Department of Defense[?], *JP 3-0: Joint Operations* ([Washington D.C.?], 11 August 2011), II-5.

sustained operations to achieve U.S. strategic and political goals in a broad geographic region. Finally, the importance of facilities was stressed throughout this monograph; these facilities directly affect the *operational reach* of U.S. forces. Sufficient facilities will extend the operational reach of U.S. forces, and help prevent *culmination* before the military end state is reached.

A number of additional trends are worth noting. First, in the two historical cases, political and strategic objectives were unclear to varying degrees. This has ramifications for the Arctic as well. Due to the nature of the potential threats in the region, and the lack of an existential threat, policy guidance regarding the region is likely to remain broad in nature. The lack of a clear threat combined with limited resources could contribute to an approach of reacting to major changes in the Arctic, rather than being proactive. In this light, applying the lessons learned and understanding gained from the first two case studies may be useful in informing planners for the Arctic region.

Second, the importance of considering the Navy, and later the Air Force, in formulating strategy is apparent when focusing on regions dominated by oceans, seas, and littoral regions. This dynamic is likely to echo in the Arctic. U.S. Army and Marine forces can certainly operate in the Arctic; but, the nature of the environment, the vagueness and nature of the potential threats, and the potential difficulty of using ground forces to achieve strategic and political objects in the Arctic suggest that U.S leaders will most heavily draw on the U.S. Air Force, Coast Guard, and Navy in this particular region in the future.

Finally, the challenge of projecting forces across vast distances is apparent in all three cases. Planners in the first two case studies seemed to successfully construct lines of communications (LOCs) to effectively support these operations. And the Arctic is no exception when it comes to the importance of LOCs to support operations. In fact, it could be more important due to the potential need to support operations in multiple areas of the Arctic requiring separate LOCs.

Chapter V: Conclusion and Recommendations

This monograph addressed the question of whether an increase in U.S. military responsibility in a geographic region—a geo-environmental change—leads to an increase in operational risk. This hypothesis was analyzed using Doctrine, Organization, Technology, Threat, and Facilities as the intervening variables. In the two historical case studies examined, the operational risk as a whole increased when analyzed through the DOTTF variables. For various reasons, including limited resources, unclear strategic guidance, and other issues in adapting to the geo-environmental changes, the U.S. government was either unable to adequately overcome the challenges (in the case of the Asia–Pacific region in the early 1900s), or it was unclear whether the United States had adequately addressed them (in the Indian Ocean region). This monograph then applied these lessons to a contemporary challenge—the geo-environmental change for United States military forces that appears to be occurring in the Arctic region. The unclear nature of the potential threats, the challenges involved with Arctic operations, the potential for interservice rivalry in an period of limited resources, and the broad stated political and strategic objectives suggest a significant challenge ahead for operational planners in that region.

The analysis suggests that the facilities variable was the most important in reducing operational risk for U.S. forces in geo-environmental changes. In this light, it would be prudent for U.S. leaders to closely analyze how facilities and infrastructure might best support the future projection of forces into the region in response to a wide variety of contingencies.[313] It is true that, as noted by the DoD, facilities construction in the Arctic requires "long lead times," is difficult in practice, and expensive;[314] however, the importance of this variable in historical cases of geo-

---

[313] As laid out by the Department of Defense: Department of Defense, *Report to Congress,* 29–32.

[314] Department of Defense, *Report to Congress*, 24–25.

environmental change should not be ignored. The U.S. should weigh the difficulties and the monetary costs of construction against the security costs of postponing facilities and infrastructure decisions—especially in light of the historical lessons provided here.

This monograph suggests that, in general, clear answers are not on the immediate horizon for the military's operational planners concerned with the Arctic. However, applying the lessons learned and understanding gained from the historical case studies examined here may be useful in informing operational planners about the Arctic region in the years ahead.

BIBLIOGRAPHY

Books and Book Chapters

Beazley, Kim C. "The October War, the 1973–1974 Arab Oil Embargo, and U.S. Policy on the Indian Ocean." In Bowman and Clark, 107–129.

Bezboruah, Monoranjan. *U.S. Strategy in the Indian Ocean: The International Response*. Praeger: New York, 1977.

Bowman, Larry W., and Jeffrey A. Lefebvre. "The Indian Ocean: U.S. Military and Strategic Perspectives." In Dowdy and Trood, 413–435.

Bowman, Larry W., and Ian Clark, eds. *The Indian Ocean in Global Politics*. Boulder: Westview Press, 1981.

Braisted, William Reynolds. *The United States Navy in the Pacific, 1897–1909*. New York: Greenwood Press, 1969.

———. *The United States Navy in the Pacific, 1909–1922*. Austin: University of Texas, 1971.

Braun, Dieter, translated by Carol Geldart and Kathleen Llanwarne. *The Indian Ocean: Region of Conflict or "Peace Zone"?* New York: St. Martin's Press, 1983.

Cottrell, Alvin J., and R.M. Burrell, eds. *The Indian Ocean: Its Political, Economic, and Military Importance*. New York: Praeger, 1972.

Cottrell, Alvin J. and Walter F. Hahn, *Indian Ocean Naval Limitations: Regional Issues and Global Implications*. New York: National Strategy Information Center, 1976.

Dockrill, Saki. *Britain's Retreat from East of Suez: The Choice between Europe and the World?* Houndmills, Basingstoke, Hampshire [U.K.?]: Palgrave MacMillan, 2002.

Dowdy, William L., and Russell B. Trood, eds. *The Indian Ocean: Perspectives on a Strategic Arena*. Durham: Duke University Press, 1985.

Gaddis, John Lewis. *Surprise, Security, and the American Experience*. Cambridge: Harvard University Press, 2005.

Gordon, Sandy, with Desmond Ball, Paul Dibb, and Amin Saikal. *Security and Security Building in the Indian Ocean Region*. Canberra: Strategic and Defence Studies Centre, 1996.

Hendrix, Henry J. *Theodore Roosevelt's Naval Diplomacy: The U.S. Navy and the Birth of the American Century*. Annapolis: Naval Institute Press, 2009.

Kapur, Ashok. "Carter's Diplomacy and the Indian Ocean Region." In Bowman and Clark, 131–148.

Knox, MacGregor, and Williamson Murray, eds. *The Dynamics of Military Revolution 1300–2050*. New York: Cambridge University Press, 2009.

Kretchik, Walter E. *U.S. Army Doctrine: From the American Revolution to the War on Terror*. Lawrence, Kansas: University Press of Kansas, 2011.

Linn, Brian McAllister. *Guardians of Empire: The U.S. Army and the Pacific, 1902–1940*. Chapel Hill: University of North Carolina Press, 1997.

Mandeles, Mark D. *Military Transformation Past and Present: Historical Lessons for the 21st Century*. Connecticut: Praeger Security International, 2007.

Murray, Williamson, and MacGregor Knox, "Thinking about Revolutions in Warfare." In Knox and Murray, 1–14.

Murray, Williamson, and Allan R. Millett, eds. *Military Innovation in the Interwar Period.* New York: Cambridge University Press, 2009.

Rais, Rasul B. *The Indian Ocean and the Superpowers.* New Jersey: Barnes & Noble Press, 1987.

Rogers, Clifford J. " 'As If a New Sun had Arisen': England's Fourteenth-century RMA." In Knox and Murray, 15–34.

Tahtinen, Dale R., and John Lenczowski. *Arms in the Indian Ocean: Interests and Challenges.* Washington D.C.: American Enterprise Institute for Public Policy Research, 1977.

Vine, David. *Island of Shame: The Secret History of the U.S. Military Base on Diego Garcia.* Princeton: Princeton University Press, 2009.

von Clausewitz, Carl, in Michael Howard and Peter Paret, (eds. and trans.). *On War.* Indexed Edition. Princeton: Princeton University Press, 1984.

Weeks, Stanley B., and Charles A. Meconis. *The Armed Forces of the USA in the Asia–Pacific Region.* New York: I.B. Taurus, 1999.

Wriggins, Howard. "U.S. Interests in the Indian Ocean." In Cottrell and Burell, 357–377.

Journal Articles

Berlin, Donald L. "Neglected No Longer: Strategic Rivalry in the Indian Ocean." *Harvard International Review* (Summer 2002): 26–31.

Borgerson, Scott G. "Arctic Meltdown: The Economic and Security Implications of Global Warming," *Foreign Affairs* (March/April 2008), http://www.foreignaffairs.com/articles/63222/scott-g-borgerson/arctic-meltdown (accessed 4 February 2012): 63–77.

Bronfeld, Saul. "Did TRADOC Outmanoeuvre the Manoeuvrists? A Comment." *War & Society* 27. No 2 (October 2008): 111–125. http://www.tase.co.il/NR/rdonlyres/29165C6B-875F-4B92-ACFA-4ACC3739CAD0/0/Did_TRADOC_Outmanoeuvre_the_Manoeuvrists_s.pdf (accessed 15 February 2012).

Dahl, Erik J. "Naval Innovation: From Coal to Oil." *Joint Forces Quarterly* (Winter 2000–2001): 50–56.

Fitch, George Hamlin. "The New Pacific Empire," *The World's Work III* (November 1901–April 1902): 1591–1597.

Kimball, Jeffrey. "The Nixon Doctrine: A Saga of Misunderstanding." *Presidential Studies Quarterly* 36:1 (March 2006): 59–74. http://proquest.umi.com.lumen.cgsccarl.com/pqdlink?vinst=PROD&fmt=6&startpage=-1&vname=PQD&RQT=309&did=996135961&scaling=FULL&vtype=PQD&rqt=309&cfc=1&TS=1329363739&clientId=5094 (accessed 15 February 2012).

Russell, Anthony L. "Carpe Diem: Seizing Strategic Opportunity in the Arctic." *Joint Forces Quarterly* 51 (4th QTR 2008): 94–101.

Schierbrand, Wolf Von. "The Coming Supremacy of the Pacific: Sixth Paper—The Need of a Large Navy." *The Pacific Monthly* (January 1906): 98–101.

Young, Oran R. "The Arctic in Play: Governance in a Time of Rapid Change." *The International Journal of Marine and Coastal Law* 24 (2009): 423–442.

———. "Whither the Arctic? Conflict or Cooperation in the Circumpolar North." *Polar Record* 45: 232 (2009): 73–82.

Theses, Monographs, and Stand-alone Works

Abboud, Dave. "Safeguarding Canadian Arctic Sovereignty Against Conventional Threats." Thesis, Command and General Staff School, 2009.

Abell, Tarn M. "Arctic Security in a Warming World." Strategy Research Project, U.S. Army War College, 23 March 2010.

Department of the Army. *ATTP 3-97.11: Cold Region Operations.* Washington D.C.: Headquarters, Department of the Army, 28 January 2011.

———. *FM 3-0: Operations (with Change 1).* Washington D.C.: Headquarters, Department of the Army, February 2008 (Change 1: 22 February 2011).

———. *FM 5-0: The Operations Process.* Washington D.C.: Headquarters, Department of the Army, March 2010.

Department of Defense. *JP 1-02: Department of Defense Dictionary of Military and Associated Terms.* [Washington D.C.?]: 8 November 2010, As Amended Through 15 August 2011.

———. JP *3-0: Joint Operations.* [Washington D.C.?]: 11 August 2011.

Gibson, Robert D. "Space Power, *The* Revolution in Military Affairs." Strategy Research Project, US. Army War College, 2001.

McCarthy, Jr., Thomas R. "Global Warming Threatens National Interests in the Arctic." Strategy Research Project, U.S. Army War College, 2009.

O'Rourke, Ronald. *Changes in the Arctic: Background and Issues for Congress.* CRS Report for Congress. Washington D.C.: Congressional Research Service, 7 April 2011.

———. *Coast Guard Polar Icebreaker Modernization: Background, Issues, and Options for Congress.* CRS Report for Congress. Washington D.C.: Congressional Research Service, 21 April 2011.

Pate, Chad P. "Easing the Arctic Tension: An Economic Solution." Thesis, Naval Postgraduate School, December 2010.

Penn, Dennis R. "Africa Command and the Militarization of U.S. Foreign Policy." Strategy Research Project, U.S. Army War College, 2008.

Trent, Packard C. "An Evaluation of the Arctic—Will it Become an Area of Cooperation or Conflict?" Thesis, Naval Postgraduate School, March 2011.

Web Resources

AMAP (Arctic Monitoring and Assessment Programme) Secretariat. "Snow, Water, Ice and Permafrost in the Arctic." 2011. http://s3.documentcloud.org/documents/88367/arctic-ice-melt-2011-executivesummary.pdf (accessed 11 September 2011).

AMAP Secretariat. "AMAP: Arctic Monitoring and Assessment Programme." 2003.
http://www.amap.no/ (accessed 11 September 2011).

Arctic Council. "About the Arctic Council." 7 April 2011. http://www.arctic-council.org/index.php/en/about (accessed 4 December 2011).

Argitis, Theophilos. "Arctic Cabinet Meeting Risks New Cold War for Oil (Update1)."
Bloomberg. 26 August 2008.
http://www.bloomberg.com/apps/news?pid=21070001&sid=asUCKdhefIg4 (accessed 19 January 2012).

Bird, Kenneth J., Ronald R. Charpentier, Donald L. Gautier, David W. Houseknecht, Timothy R. Klett, Janet K. Pitman, Thomas E. Moore, Christopher J. Schenk, Marilyn E. Tennyson, and Craig J. Wandrey. "Circum-Arctic Resource Appraisal: Estimates of Undiscovered Oil and Gas North of the Arctic Circle." (USGS Fact Sheet 2008-3049). *USGS*. 23 July 2008. http://pubs.usgs.gov/fs/2008/3049/ (accessed 7 February 2012).

Boslough, Mark, Mark Ivey, Mark Taylor, Bernard Zak, and George Backus. "The Arctic as a Test Case for an Assessment of Climate Impacts on National Security." *Sandia*. November 2008. http://est.sandia.gov/earth/docs/SAND2008-7006.pdf (accessed 11 September 2011).

Conley, Heather, and Jamie Kraut. "U.S. Strategic Interests in the Arctic: An Assessment of Current Challenges and New Opportunities for Cooperation." *Center for Strategic and International Studies*. April 2010.
http://csis.org/files/publication/100426_Conley_USStrategicInterests_Web.pdf (accessed 11 September 2011).

Department of Defense. *CJCSI (Chairman of the Joint Chiefs of Staff Instruction) 3170.01G: Joint Capabilities Integration and Development System*. [1 March 2009; also states that it is "current as of 7 March 2011"].
http://www.dtic.mil/cjcs_directives/cdata/unlimit/3170_01.pdf (accessed 11 September 2011).

———. *Report to Congress on Arctic Operations and the Northwest Passage*. DoD Report to Congress. May 2011.
http://www.defense.gov/pubs/pdfs/Tab_A_Arctic_Report_Public.pdf (accessed 13 September 2011).

———. *Sustaining U.S. Global Leadership: Priorities for 21st Century Defense*.
www.defense.gov. 5 January 2012.
http://www.defense.gov/news/Defense_Strategic_Guidance.pdf (accessed 19 January 2012).

Garamone, Jim. "Unified Command Plan Reflects Arctic's Importance." Defense.gov. 7 April 2011. http://www.defense.gov/news/newsarticle.aspx?id=63467 (accessed 3 December 2011).

Heubert, Rob. *The Newly Emerging Arctic Security Environment*. *Canadian Defence and Foreign Affairs Institute*. March 2010.
http://www.cdfai.org/PDF/The%20Newly%20Emerging%20Arctic%20Security%20Environment.pdf (accessed 12 September 2011).

Kaplan, Robert D. "Center Stage for the Twenty-First Century: Power Plays in the Indian Ocean." *Foreign Affairs*, 88:2. 2009: 16+. *Academic OneFile*.
http://go.galegroup.com.lumen.cgsccarl.com/ps/i.do?&id=GALE%7CA194963208&v=2.1&u=97mwrlib&it=r&p=AONE&sw=w (accessed 30 October 2011).

Martin Kaste. "In The Arctic Race, The U.S. Lags Behind." August 19, 2011.
http://www.npr.org/2011/08/19/139681324/in-the-arctic-race-the-u-s-lags-behind
(accessed 1 December 2011).

Kristiansen, Ivar. "The Role of Pan-Arctic Bodies." *Conference of Parliamentarians of the Arctic Region.* 22 January 2007.
http://www.arcticparl.org/files/images/speech%20Kristiansen%20Arctic%20Frontiers.pdf (accessed 12 January 2012).

Macalister, Terry. "US and Russia Stir Up Political Tensions Over Arctic." 6 July 2011.
http://www.guardian.co.uk/world/2011/jul/06/us-russia-political-tensions-arctic (accessed 14 January 2012).

Nixon, Richard. "Informal Remarks in Guam With Newsmen." 25 July 1969. *The American Presidency Project* (by Gerhard Peters and John T. Woolley)
http://www.presidency.ucsb.edu/ws/?pid=2140 (accessed 16 February2012).

Reid, Tim. "Arctic Military Bases Signal New Cold War." *Times* [London, England] 11 Aug. 2007: 39. *Academic OneFile.* Web. 11 February 2011.

Theophilos Argitis, "Arctic Cabinet Meeting Risks New Cold War for Oil (Update1)." Bloomberg. 26 August 2008.
http://www.bloomberg.com/apps/news?pid=21070001&sid=asUCKdhefIg4 (accessed 19 January 2012).

United States. *National Security Strategy.* White House. 2010.
http://www.whitehouse.gov/sites/default/files/rss_viewer/national_security_strategy.pdf (accessed 4 December 2011).

United States Navy. "Chief of Naval Operations (CNO) Admiral Gary Roughhead speaks at Active in the Arctic Seminar." www.navy.mil. 16 June 2011.
http://www.navy.mil/navydata/people/cno/Roughead/Speech/110616%20Arctic%20Capitol%20Hill.pdf (accessed 13 September 2011).

U.S. Geological Survey. "90 Billion Barrels of Oil and 1,670 Trillion Cubic Feet of Natural Gas Assessed in the Arctic." 23 July 2008.
http://www.usgs.gov/newsroom/article.asp?ID=1980&from=rss_home (accessed 12 September 2011).

www.ingramcontent.com/pod-product-compliance
Lightning Source LLC
Chambersburg PA
CBHW080515290526
45790CB00006B/2172